SIXTH EDITION

INTERACTIONS 2

Reading

TEACHER'S MANUAL WITH TESTS

Pamela Hartmann
Elaine Kirn

Teacher's Manual by
Carol Pineiro

McGraw Hill

Interactions 2 Reading, Teacher's Manual with Tests, Sixth Edition

Published by McGraw-Hill ESL/ELT, a business unit of The McGraw-Hill Companies, Inc. 1221 Avenue of the Americas, New York, NY 10020.

Some ancillaries, including electronic and print components, may not be available to customers outside the United States.

This book is printed on acid-free paper.

1 2 3 4 5 6 7 8 9 0 TK/TK 1 0 9 8 7 6 5 4 3 2
ISBN: 978-1-10-792196-2
MHID: 1-25-907061-1

Senior Vice President, Products & Markets: Kurt L. Strand
Vice President, General Manager, Products & Markets: Michael J. Ryan
Vice President, Content Production & Technology Services: Kimberly Meriwether David
Director of Development: Valerie Kelemen
Marketing Manager: Cambridge University Press
Lead Project Manager: Rick Hecker
Senior Buyer: Michael R. McCormick
Designer: Page2, LLC
Cover/Interior Designer: Page2, LLC
Senior Content Licensing Specialist: Keri Johnson
Manager, Digital Production: Janean A. Utley
Compositor: Page2, LLC
Printer: Yurchak

Cover photo: Rechitan Sorin/Shutterstock.com

www.mhhe.com

McGraw-Hill ELT

www.elt.mcgraw-hill.com

The McGraw-Hill Companies

Table of Contents

Welcome to the Teacher's Manual

The Teacher's Manual of *Interactions/Mosaic* provides support and flexibility to teachers using the *Interactions/Mosaic* 18-book academic skills series. The Teacher's Manual provides step-by-step guidance for implementing each activity in the Student Book. The Teacher's Manual also provides expansion activities with photocopiable masters of select expansion activities, identification of activities that support a Best Practice, valuable notes on content, answer keys, audioscripts, end-of-chapter tests, and placement tests. Each chapter in the Teacher's Manual begins with an overview of the content, vocabulary, and teaching goals in that chapter. Each chapter in the Student Book begins with an engaging photo and related discussion questions that strengthen the educational experience and connect students to the topic.

- **Procedural Notes**
  The procedural notes are useful for both experienced and new teachers. Experienced teachers can use the bulleted, step-by step procedural notes as a quick guide and refresher before class, while newer or substitute teachers can use the notes as a more extensive guide to assist them in the classroom. The procedural notes guide teachers through each strategy and activity; describe what materials teachers might need for an activity; and help teachers provide context for the activities.

- **Answer Keys**
  Answer keys are provided for all activities that have definite answers. For items that have multiple correct answers, various possible answers are provided. The answer key follows the procedural note for the relevant activity. Answer keys are also provided for the Chapter Tests and the Placement Tests.

- **Expansion Activities**
  A number of expansion activities with procedural notes are included in each chapter. These activities offer teachers creative ideas for reinforcing the chapter content while appealing to different learning styles. Activities include games, conversation practice, presentations, and projects. These expansion activities often allow students to practice integrated language skills, not just the skills that the student book focuses on. Some of the expansion activities include photocopiable black line masters included in the back of the book.

- **Content Notes**
  Where appropriate, content notes are included in the Teacher's Manual. These are notes that might illuminate or enhance a learning point in the activity and might help teachers answer student questions about the content. These notes are provided at the logical point of use, but teachers can decide if and when to use the information in class.

- **Chapter Tests**
  Each chapter includes a chapter test that was designed to test the vocabulary, reading, writing, grammar, and/or listening strategies taught in the chapter, depending on the language skill strand being used. Teachers can simply copy and distribute the tests, then use the answer keys found in the Teacher's Manual. The purpose of the chapter tests is not only to assess students' understanding of material covered in the chapter but also to give students an idea of how they are doing and what they need to work on. Each chapter test has four parts with items totaling 100 points. Item types include multiple choice, fill-in-the blank, and true/false. Audioscripts are provided when used.

- **Black Line Masters (Photocopiable Masters)**
  Each chapter includes a number of expansion activities with black line masters, or master worksheets, that teachers can copy and distribute. These activities and black line masters are

optional. They can help reinforce and expand on chapter material in an engaging way. Activities include games; conversation practice; working with manipulatives such as sentence strips; projects; and presentations. Procedural notes and answer keys (when applicable) are provided in the Teacher's Manual.

- **Placement Tests**
  Each of the four language skill strands has a placement test designed to help assess in which level the student belongs. Each test has been constructed to be given in under an hour. Be sure to go over the directions and answer any questions before the test begins. Students are instructed not to ask questions once the test begins. Following each placement test, you'll find a scoring placement key that suggests the appropriate book to be used based on the number of items answered correctly. Teachers should use judgment in placing students and selecting texts.

The Interactions/Mosaic Program

Interactions/Mosaic is a fully-integrated, 18-book academic skills series. Language proficiencies are articulated from the beginning through advance levels within each of the four language skill strands. Chapter themes articulate across the four skill strands to systematically recycle content, vocabulary, and grammar.

- **Reading Strand**
  Reading skills and strategies are strategically presented and practiced through a variety of themes and reading genres in the five Reading books. Pre-reading, reading, and post-reading activities include strategies and activities that aid comprehension, build vocabulary, and prepare students for academic success. Each chapter includes at least two readings that center around the same theme, allowing students to deepen their understanding of a topic and command of vocabulary related to that topic. Readings include magazine articles, textbook passages, essays, letters, and website articles. They explore, and guide the student to explore, stimulating topics. Vocabulary is presented before each reading and is built on throughout the chapter. High-frequency words and words from the Academic Word List are focused on and pointed out with asterisks (*) in each chapter's Self-Assessment Log.

- **Listening/Speaking Strand**
  A variety of listening input, including lectures, academic discussions, and conversations help students explore stimulating topics in the five Listening/Speaking books. Activities associated with the listening input, such as pre-listening tasks, systematically guide students through strategies and critical thinking skills that help prepare them for academic achievement. In the Interactions books, the activities are coupled with instructional photos featuring a cast of engaging, multi-ethnic students participating in North American college life. Across the strand, lectures and dialogues are broken down into manageable parts giving students an opportunity to predict, identify main ideas, and effectively manage lengthy input. Questions, guided discussion activities, and structured pair and group work stimulate interest and interaction among students, often culminating in organizing their information and ideas in a graphic organizer, writing, and/or making a presentation to the class. Pronunciation is highlighted in every chapter, an aid to improving both listening comprehension and speaking fluency. Enhanced focus on vocabulary building is developed throughout and a list of target words for each chapter is provided so students can interact meaningfully with the material. Finally, Online Learning Center features MP3 files from the Student Book audio program for students to download onto portable digital audio players.

- **Writing Strand**
  Activities in each of the four Writing books are systematically structured to culminate in a *Writing Product* task. Activities build on key elements of writing from sentence development to writing single paragraphs, articles, narratives, and essays of multiple lengths and genres. Connections between writing and grammar tie the writing skill in focus with the grammar structures needed to develop each writing skill. Academic themes, activities, writing topics, vocabulary development, and critical thinking strategies prepare students for university life. Instructional photos are used to strengthen engagement and the educational experience. Explicit pre-writing questions and discussions activate prior knowledge, help organize ideas and information, and create a foundation for the writing product. Each chapter includes a self-evaluation rubric which supports the learner as he or she builds confidence and autonomy in academic writing. Finally, the Writing Articulation Chart helps teachers see the progression of writing strategies both in terms of mechanics and writing genres.

- **Grammar Strand**
  Questions and topical quotes in the four Grammar books, coupled with instructional photos stimulate interest, activate prior knowledge, and launch the topic of each chapter. Engaging academic topics provide context for the grammar and stimulate interest in content as well as grammar. A variety of activity types, including individual, pair, and group work, allow students to build grammar skills and use the grammar they are learning in activities that cultivate critical thinking skills. Students can refer to grammar charts to review or learn the form and function of each grammar point. These charts are numbered sequentially, formatted consistently, and indexed systematically, providing lifelong reference value for students.

- **Focus on Testing for the TOEFL® iBT**
  The TOEFL® iBT *Focus on Testing* sections prepare students for success on the TOEFL® iBT by presenting and practicing specific strategies for each language skill area. The Focus on Testing sections are introduced in Interactions 1 and are included in all subsequent levels of the Reading, Listening/Speaking, and Writing strands. These strategies focus on what The Educational Testing Service (ETS) has identified as the target skills in each language skill area. For example, "reading for basic comprehension" (identifying the main idea, understanding pronoun reference) is a target reading skill and is presented and practiced in one or more *Focus on Testing* sections. In addition, this and other target skills are presented and practiced in chapter components outside the *Focus on Testing* sections and have special relevance to the TOEFL® iBT. For example, note-taking is an important testtaking strategy, particularly in the listening section of the TOEFL® iBT, and is included in activities within each of the Listening/Speaking books. All but two of the *Interactions/Mosaic* titles have a *Focus on Testing* section. Although *Interactions Access Reading* and *Interaction Access Listening/Speaking* don't include these sections because of their level, they do present and develop skills that will prepare students for the TOEFL® iBT.

- **Best Practices**
  In each chapter of this Teacher's Manual, you'll find Best Practices boxes that highlight a particular activity and show how this activity is tied to a particular Best Practice. The team of writers, editors, and teacher consultants has identified the following six interconnected Best Practices.

* TOEFL® is a registered trademark of Educational Testing Services (ETS). This product is not endorsed or approved by ETS.

Interactions/Mosaic Best Practices

Best Practices

Each chapter identifies at least six different activities that support six Best Practices, principles that contribute to excellent language teaching and learning. Identifying Best Practices helps teachers to see, and make explicit for students, how a particular activity will aid the learning process.

Making Use of Academic Content

Materials and tasks based on academic content and experiences give learning real purpose. Students explore real world issues, discuss academic topics, and study content-based and thematic materials.

Organizing Information

Students learn to organize thoughts and notes through a variety of graphic organizers that accommodate diverse learning and thinking styles.

Scaffolding Instruction

A scaffold is a physical structure that facilitates construction of a building. Similarly, scaffolding instruction is a tool used to facilitate language learning in the form of predictable and flexible tasks. Some examples include oral or written modeling by the teacher or students, placing information in a larger framework, and reinterpretation.

Activating Prior Knowledge

Students can better understand new spoken or written material when they connect to the content. Activating prior knowledge allows students to tap into what they already know, building on this knowledge, and stirring a curiosity for more knowledge.

Interacting with Others

Activities that promote human interaction in pair work, small group work, and whole class activities present opportunities for real world contact and real world use of language.

Critical Thinking

Strategies for critical thinking are taught explicitly. Students learn tools that promote critical thinking skills crucial to success in the academic world.

CHAPTER 1

Education and Student Life

In this CHAPTER

Students will read about educational systems in Finland, Korea, Singapore, and the United States. Discussing and debating the similarities and differences among these systems will allow students to compare and contrast what they know and have learned about other educational systems. They will also read articles with specific suggestions and solutions to the challenges of the first year of college.

> "An education isn't how much you have committed to memory, or even how much you know. It's being able to differentiate between what you do know and what you don't."
>
> Anatole France
> French author

Chapter Opener

- Read the introductory paragraph explaining what students will be doing in this chapter.
- Direct student's attention to the photo on pages 2–3. Ask them to describe whom they see and what the people are doing. What are they waiting for? (possibly an exam)
- Ask about exams that your students have taken and how they felt before, during, and after the exams.
- Discuss what students think is important in education and what helps them be successful.
- Draw students' attention to the quotation at the bottom of page 2. Point out that Anatole France lived from 1844 to 1924. Ask students if they think the definition of education has changed since that time. Also ask students for their opinions about the quotation.

Chapter Overview

Reading Selections

The Secrets of Success in School

Challenges of the First Year of College

Reading Skills and Strategies

Previewing the topic and vocabulary

Identifying the main idea

Understanding reading structure

Skimming for the topic and main idea

Critical-Thinking Skills

Organizing information using a T-chart and Venn diagram

Summarizing a paragraph

Finding information about schools online

Vocabulary Building

Getting meaning from context: punctuation, other sentences, logic

Focusing on the Academic Word List

Recognizing word meanings

Identifying words and phrases that work together

Language Skills

Understanding pronoun reference

Discussing educational systems in different cultures

Writing a paragraph

Focusing on Testing TOEFL® iBT

Focusing on question types

Vocabulary

Nouns
- assignments*
- credits*
- curriculum
- discipline
- drawback
- effort
- exhaustion
- rankings
- resources*
- secondary school
- status*
- values

Verbs
- achieve*
- compare
- determine
- reflect
- required*
- schedule*
- separate
- track

Adjectives
- challenging*
- competitive
- entire
- global*
- identical*
- isolated*
- obvious*
- universal

Adverb
- finally*

Expressions
- in contrast to
- one-size-fits-all
- on the one hand
- on the other hand
- the best and the brightest

*These words are from the Academic Word List. For more information on this list, see www.victoria.ac.nz/lals/resources/academicwordlist/

The Secrets of Success in School

Before You Read

1 Previewing the Topic

- Put students in small groups and have them look at the photos. Tell them to practice asking and answering the questions.
- Call on students to share their answers with the class. Their answers may vary.
- Write a few comments they may have about the photos on the board. If there are students from those countries in class, ask them to add their comments.
- Have students look up the full list of countries that participate in the PISA exam.

Expansion Activity

REPRODUCIBLE

- Photocopy and distribute **Black Line Master 1** "Can You Tell Me About Your Schooling?" on page BLM1 of this Teacher's Manual.
- Model the activity. Call on a student and ask: *"In what city or town and in what country did you go to elementary school? Was it public or private?"* Point out that they should write their partner's answers on the paper.
- Divide students into pairs of students from different countries or regions, if possible.
- Write the beginning and ending time on the board. Students should be able to complete this activity in 10–15 minutes.
- Walk around the room and help students with the questions, if necessary.
- At the end of the time limit, ask the pairs of students to introduce each other to the class.

2 Previewing Vocabulary

- Read the directions to students.
- Have them read the words and phrases to themselves. Then play the audio so that they can hear the pronunciation.
- Tell students to put a check mark (✓) next to the words they know.
- Tell students **not** to use a dictionary during this part of the lesson.

Strategy

Getting Meaning from Context

- On the board, put the phrase *Clues to Meaning*. Under it, write the following punctuation marks (words and symbols) and expressions:

  parentheses ( ) dash (—) comma (,)

  ❑ Another sentence before or after the word or phrase may help.

  ❑ Logic may also help you guess.
- Tell students to look for these punctuation marks and clues when they see words or phrases they don't understand. These clues to meaning will help them understand new words and phrases. Read the examples and explain further if necessary.

3 Getting Meaning from Context

- Tell student to do the activity.
- If students finish quickly, have them compare their answers with a partner.

ANSWER KEY

1. on the one hand = from one point of view; on the other hand = from another point of view
2. identical = the same
3. drawback = disadvantage
4. status = social position
5. determines = decides
6. reflects = mirrors, shows

Read

4 Reading an Article

- Write *"What can we learn from countries with successful educational systems?"* on the board. Tell students to think about this question as they are reading.
- Have students read the passage silently within a time limit (10 minutes) or have students follow along silently as you play the audio.
- Tell students to underline any words or phrases that are new or that they don't understand. Remind them **not** to use a dictionary during this part of the lesson.
- Tell students to read the Strategy: Identifying the Main Idea, on page 8, if they finish before the other students.

ANSWER KEY

Answers may vary.

Paragraph A: Because the global economy is becoming more competitive, educators and governments worldwide are paying close attention to these tests to find out their countries compare—and to learn how they can improve.

Paragraph F: There is no magic solution, but in this global economy, no educational system is isolated from others, and each *can* learn from others.

After You Read

Strategy

Identifying the Main Idea

- Call on a student to read aloud the information in the box.
- Provide a visual of the Strategy by drawing an umbrella on the board. Write the words *Main Idea* on the umbrella. Using a well-known story as an example (such as a fable), write specific ideas and details under the umbrella.

5 Identifying the Main Idea

- Read the directions and have students look at Paragraphs A and F and write down the main idea.
- If students finish quickly, have them compare their answers with a partner.

6 Understanding Reading Structure

- Read the directions. Tell students to look back at the reading on pages 6–8 and match the paragraphs with their topics.
- Check the answers as a class.

ANSWER KEY

1. F **2.** C **3.** E **4.** B **5.** D **6.** A

7 Checking Your Vocabulary

- Read the directions. Remind students **not** to use a dictionary during this part of the lesson.
- Check the answers when students finish.

ANSWER KEY

1. competitive	**7.** the best and the brightest
2. compare	**8.** contrast
3. track	**9.** universal
4. separate	**10.** entire
5. effort	**11.** values
6. rankings	**12.** Isolated

Strategy

Organizing Information: Using a T-Chart and a Venn Diagram

- Point out the words and expressions that are highlighted in the Strategy box that show contrasting viewpoints: *advantages, disadvantages, on the one hand, on the other hand, but, however.*
- Have students repeat them after you.
- Read the information describing a T-chart and a Venn diagram. Explain that in the next activity, students will use a T-chart and a Venn diagram to organize information from the reading.

8 Organizing Information: Using Graphic Organizers

Best Practice

Organizing Information

Activities such as this will teach students to organize information from a reading passage using a T-chart and a Venn diagram. Using graphic organizers allows students to better assimilate and recall information at a later date, making it a valuable student tool. In this case, students identify the features and the similarities and differences of the educational systems of the countries mentioned in the reading.

- Read the directions. Divide students into pairs and have each pair fill out the two T-charts on page 10.
- Give students a time limit (10 minutes) and check the answers with the whole class when everyone has finished the T-charts.
- Draw a Venn diagram on the board like the one on page 11. Explain to students that in this graphic organizer, they identify the features that are the same in the two countries, Korea and Finland, in the overlapping part of the ovals. The differences in the two educational systems go in the outside sections of the ovals.
- Have students work together with their partners to complete the Venn diagram.
- Have volunteers fill in the Venn diagram on the board.

ANSWER KEY

Answers may vary.

Paragraph B T-chart

Singapore: tracking students by ability, different groups go to different jobs

Finland: all students learn together, successful students serve as examples to weaker students

Paragraph E T-chart

Finland and Korea: universal curriculum, fewer topics

the United States: each state chooses curriculum, different subjects from state to state, many topics

Paragraphs C and D Venn diagram

Korea: many hours in school and homework, competitive

Finland: no grades until high school, little homework, non-competitive

Both: teachers have high status; teachers are of high quality

Culture Note

What Do You Think?

Can the Finnish, Korean, or Singaporean system transfer to other countries?

- Have students listen as you read the Culture Note and take notes. You may wish to put the discussion question on the board: *Can the Finnish, Korean, or Singaporean system transfer to other countries?*
- Ask students to present their opinions on the discussion questions. Ask them to include observations from their own countries or other countries they know.
- Encourage students to use phrases like: *In my opinion…, Based on my experience…, I agree with you; however, …* , to introduce their point of view.

9 Discussing the Reading

Best Practice

Activating Prior Knowledge

Activities such as this will connect new concepts to students' prior knowledge. By making connections between the text and their own experiences, students will be better able to understand the reading and reflect on their own schooling in light of it. By working in a small group, students will help each other make those connections and learn from the group. Finally, by presenting their conclusions to the class they will share their knowledge and culture with others.

- Divide students into small groups from the same country or region, if possible.
- Have students read the questions on page 11 and write brief answers.
- When they finish, ask them to go to the board and make an outline of their school system, or put the outline on a chart.
- Have students give a short presentation to the class. Those in the audience can take notes and ask questions at the end. Hang the charts around the classroom when students are finished.

Challenges of the First Year of College

Before You Read

Strategy

Skimming for the Topic and Main Idea

- Be sure students understand the difference between the topic and the main idea of a paragraph.
- Have students review the Hint box in the side margin.
- Read the Example passage aloud to students or call on student volunteers to each read a few sentences.
- Ask students to tell you the topic and the main idea.
- If necessary, have students do an additional example, using one or more paragraphs from the reading on pages 6–8.

Read

1 Skimming for the Topic and the Main Idea

- Tell students to read the paragraphs quickly and write the topic and main idea of each paragraph.
- Remind them **not** to use a dictionary.
- Play the audio.
- Have students check their answers with a partner if they finish quickly.

ANSWER KEY

Answers may vary.

A. Topic: challenges of college years;
Main Idea: College years can be a painful and exciting time of transition.

B. Topic: organizing for college success;
Main idea: There are six ways for students to organize themselves to work effectively and be successful.

C. Topic: money;
Main idea: Money is a problem for college students, but there are solutions.

D. Topic: depression;
Main idea: Staying connected to other is most important to avoid depression. For serious depression, professional help is needed and available.

E. Topic: benefits of college;
Main idea: Despite the challenges, college can influence the rest of the student's life.

After You Read

FOCUS

Understanding Pronoun Reference

- Explain the difference between nouns (the names of people, places, or things) and pronouns (words that take the place of a person, place, or thing). For example: *boy* = *he, chair* = *it, girl* = *she, we, you.*
- Write the following list on the board or read it aloud. Ask students to tell you if the words are nouns or pronouns. (* = pronouns)

all*	other*
campus	philosophy
classes	professor
each*	religion
entertainment	science
graduation	she*
he*	someone*
his*	style
Internet	technology
it*	them*
jobs	these*
museums	they*
none*	training
ones*	whose*

- Explain that in sentences and paragraphs, pronouns *refer* to nouns that come before them. These nouns are called *referents*, and it's important to locate them in a previous sentence or paragraph in order to understand what the reading is about.
- Direct students to the information in the Focus box on page 15 as they read the example.

2 Understanding Pronoun Reference

- Have students work individually to complete the activity.
- Review the answers with the class.

ANSWER KEY

1. these dates
2. test
3. cramming
4. students in the study group
5. the solution to the challenge of paying for college
6. students
7. credit cards
8. other people

3 Discussing the Reading

Best Practice

Scaffolding Instruction
This activity uses students' prior knowledge as a scaffold. It will help them place what they already know about their own educational system or campus life into the larger framework introduced in the reading "Challenges of the First Year of College" on pages 13–15. They will engage in "reinterpretation" or critical thinking about this topic as they formulate ideas with their classmates and give a presentation to the class.

- This activity can be conducted like **9 Discussing the Reading** on page 11, forming another part of the project on educational systems in different countries.
- Divide students into pairs from the same country or region, if possible.
- Have students read the questions on page 16 and write brief answers.
- When they finish, ask them to go to the board and make an outline of campus life and students in their country or put the outline on a chart.
- Have students give a short presentation to the class. Those in the audience can ask questions at the end. Hang the charts around the classroom when students are finished.

Responding in Writing

Strategy

Summarizing

- Ask a student to read the explanation in the Strategy box.

4 Summarizing

- Have students turn to the reading on pages 13–15.
- Ask them to skim Paragraph A on page 13.
- Review the main idea from students and write it on the board.
- Elicit important details.
- Have students write coherent sentences that summarize the paragraph. Ask for volunteers to write their summary sentences on the board.
- The summary may look like this: "Because college is a time of transition, it can be both exciting and difficult. Students are preparing for independence, adulthood, and work. There are ways to successfully deal with the challenges."
- Now have student choose Paragraph B or C from the reading and write a summary of the paragraph.
- Remind students to look at the guidelines on page 16 and not to look at the original paragraph as they write.
- When students finish, have them compare their summary with those of other students who summarized the same paragraph.

5 Writing Your Own Ideas

Best Practice

Making Use of Academic Content
Activities such as this enable students to be more successful when they work independently. With the teacher's guidance, students are able to contribute to the summary on the board. Then they are better equipped to write a summary by themselves.

- Read the topics aloud and ask who is going to write about each topic.
- Have students write a sentence with the main idea about their topic and underline it. Go around the classroom and check the sentences. Then have students write the rest of the paragraph.
- Give students 10–15 minutes for this activity. Collect their summaries when they have finished.

Talk It Over

6 Beyond the Text: Interviewing

Best Practice

Cultivating Critical Thinking

Activities such as this prepare students of real-world interactions. Interviewing, note taking, and reporting outcomes reflect college and career tasks.

- You may want to use the **Black Line Master** described here to conduct this activity.
- Alternatively, have students create their own interview sheets and follow the instructions provided for the BLM.

REPRODUCIBLE

Expansion Activity

- Photocopy and distribute **Black Line Master 2** "Can You Tell Me Your Opinion?" on page BLM2 of this Teacher's Manual.
- Model the activity by calling on a student and saying: *"Hello, my name is... and I'm interviewing people for a class assignment. Can you tell me your opinion about the positive aspects of the educational system in your country? How about the negative aspects?"*
- Tell student they should write the person's answers on the sheet.
- Give students a few days to complete this assignment.
- When it is finished, elicit answers from students in a large group format. Write the countries' names that have not been discussed in the chapter readings and list the positive and negative aspects of their educational systems. If possible, have students make comparisons with the countries that they already discussed in the chapter.

FOCUS

The Academic Word List

- Read the information in the Focus box about the "Academic Word List."
- If you have Internet access in your classroom, show students the web page for the list. If not, have them use the computer lab or home computer to access the website.

1 Focusing on Words from the Academic Word List

- Read the directions to students.
- Say the words in the list and ask students to repeat them: *assignments, challenging, credits, finally, obvious, required, resources, schedule.*
- Tell students to begin the activity and remind them to cross off the words as they use them.
- Have the class check the answers together.

ANSWER KEY

1. challenging **2.** required **3.** credits
4. assignments **5.** schedule **6.** resources
7. obvious **8.** Finally

2 Recognizing Word Meanings

- Read the directions.
- Remind students **not** to use a dictionary during this activity.
- Check the answers as a class.

ANSWER KEY

1. e **2.** j **3.** h **4.** a **5.** k **6.** l **7.** d
8. c **9.** b **10.** f **11.** i **12.** g

3 Words in Phrases

- Read the directions.
- Tell students that they should keep a vocabulary notebook of new words with a special section for words in phrases. They should review this vocabulary every week.

ANSWER KEY

1. leads to **2.** according to **3.** separate into
4. give up **5.** worry about **6.** road to
7. in common **8.** for this reason
9. in contrast to **10.** focuses on

Using the Internet

Finding Information About Schools Online

- Read the first paragraph in the box. Ask students which search engines they usually use.
- If you have Internet access in your classroom, model the steps provided in the Example.

4 Searching the Internet

- Read the instructions for Activity 4.
- If you have Internet access in the classroom, model this activity with students. Otherwise, direct them to the computer lab or their own computer.

REPRODUCIBLE

Expansion Activity

- Photocopy and distribute **Black Line Master 3** "Find a College Or University That..." on page BLM3 in this Teacher's Manual. This activity has students search for different criteria.
- If you have Internet access in the classroom, model this activity with them. Otherwise, direct them to the computer lab or their own computer.
- Point out that they can work on this individually or with a partner.
- Instruct students to write down the name of the college/university, its location, and its web address (URL) so that other students can find it. For example, Boston University, Boston, MA/USA, www.bu.edu.
- Students will then share their findings with their classmates and copy the information on their worksheet.

FOCUS TOEFL® iBT

Reading Question Types

- Read the information in the Focus box and call on different students to read the description of each of the three types of questions.

1 Practice

- Point out the examples of each type in the Practice activity.
- Remind students that the answers are found in the reading on pages 6–8.

ANSWER KEY

1. A **2.** C **3.** D

Self-Assessment Log

- Explain to students that thinking about their learning can help them decide what to focus on in their lessons and homework, and can help them chart their progress.
- The Self-Assessment Log at the end of each chapter helps students track their own strengths and weaknesses and also encourages them to take ownership of their own learning.
- Read the directions aloud and have students check vocabulary they learned in the chapter and are prepared to use.
- Have students check the strategies practiced in the chapter (or the degree to which they learned them). They have actually used all of these strategies in Chapter 1.
- Put students in small groups. Ask students to find the information or an activity related to each strategy in the chapter.
- Tell students to find definitions in the chapter for any words they did not check.
- If possible, meet privately with each student on a regular basis and review his or her assessment log. This provides an opportunity for the student to ask key questions and for you to see where additional help may be needed and to offer one-on-one encouragement.

Best Practice

Interacting with Others

Activities such as the Expansion Activity below will energize students and add excitement to the class. Since most interaction in this chapter has been dialogic or collaborative, students will enjoy a change of pace with some competitive interaction.

Expansion Activity

- Tell students to study the vocabulary for a few minutes in pairs, asking each other to spell the words aloud. Tell them they'll have a test in a few minutes.
- Instruct students to close their books. Divide them into two teams, balanced for differences like level of English, first language, culture, and gender.
- Have students go to the board, if possible, one by one. Depending on how many students there are in the class, dictate 1–2 words/phrases to each student.
- At the end of the dictation, check the board. Ask students from the other team if the words are spelled correctly. Give them a point for each correct word.
- Tally the score at the end. The team with the highest score wins.
- If it's not possible for students to go to the board, tell them to write the answers on a piece of paper.
- Collect the tests and grade them. The team with the highest score wins.

CHAPTER 2

City Life

In this
CHAPTER

Students will read about different aspects of city life, some positive and some negative. In the first reading, they will learn about an architect who became mayor of Curitiba, a small city in Brazil. Although Brazil is a country of medium development, that is, between a developing and developed country, its cities still have many problems. Students will discover how the mayor turned Curitiba into a model city that other leaders around the world have tried to emulate. In the second reading, students will learn about a phenomenon called "sick building syndrome" that often occurs in cities. Indoor air pollution causes the people inside buildings to become ill. Students will learn about solutions to this problem, which include removing pollutants and bringing in plants that can extract dangerous chemicals from the air. These topics will encourage students to think about how life in the city can be improved so that people are able to live in increasing comfort and safety.

"When you look at a city, it's like reading the hopes, aspirations, and pride of everyone who built it."

Hugh Newell Jacobsen
U.S. Architect (1929–)

Chapter Opener

- Direct students' attention to the photo. Then have students work in small groups to answer the questions in the Connecting to the Topic box. Go over the answers as a class.
- Read the quotation by Jacobsen and ask students what it means.
- Put this sentence on the board: *Life in the city is more/ less _______ than life in the country.*
- Put students in pairs to find several words or phrases to put in the blanks.
- Call on students to share their words with the class.

Chapter Overview

Reading Selections
A City That's Doing Something Right
Sick–Building Syndrome

Reading Skills and Strategies
Previewing the topic and vocabulary
Identifying the main idea
Identifying supporting details
Predicting content of a reading
Skimming for the topic and the main ideas
Scanning

Critical-Thinking Skills
Organizing details using a graphic organizer
Making inferences
Summarizing a paragraph
Understanding contrast

Vocabulary Building
Getting meaning from context: examples, opposites, and connecting words
Understanding the meaning of italics in readings
Focusing on the Academic Word List
Understanding and looking up parts of speech in a dictionary

Language Skills
Understanding pronoun reference
Interviewing students about city life
Discussing some problems and solutions in big cities
Writing a paragraph

Focus on Testing TOEFL® IBT
Getting meaning from context

Vocabulary

Nouns
- access*
- agricultural operation
- crops
- developing countries
- environment*
- gridlock
- mass transit
- pedestrian zone
- pollution
- priorities*
- produce
- recycling plant
- residents*
- transportation*
- trash
- urban dwellers

Verbs
- commute
- crowd
- cultivate
- established*
- focus*
- predict*
- solve
- worsening

Adjectives
- affluent
- creative*
- global*

Adverb
- efficiently

*These words are from the Academic Word List. For more information on this list, see www.victoria.ac.nz/lals/resources/awl.

A City That's Doing Something Right

Before You Read

1 Previewing the Topic

- Put students in pairs and have them look at the photos.
- Have students read the questions on page 24 and discuss the answers with their partner. Tell them to write adjectives to describe the photos.
- Call on students to share their answers with the class.
- Write some of the adjectives on the board and discuss their meaning.

2 Thinking Ahead

- Read the directions to the students.
- Give them a time limit for the activity (10–15 minutes).
- When they finish, have them sit down and ask them to share their answers with the class.
- Write the names of their cities on the board.
- Write down a few of the worst problems and best features.
- Point out that their lists are probably similar because many cities have similar problems and attractions.

3 Previewing Vocabulary

- Read the directions to the students.
- Have them put a check (✔) next to the words they know.
- Remind them **not** to use a dictionary during this part of the lesson.
- Tell them to put the stress on words of more than one syllable as they listen to the audio program.
- Write these words on the board as examples: *grid'lock, predict', ac'tually*
- Play the audio.
- Have the students write the words with the stress marked on the board.

ANSWER KEY

Nouns
agricultural operation
crops
developing countries
gridlock
mass transit
pedestrian zone
pollution
priorities
produce
recycling plant
trash
urban dwellers

Verbs
commute
crowd
cultivate
predict
solve
worsening

Adjectives
affluent
creative

Adverb
efficiently

Pronunciation Note

Students may be able to repeat words correctly after the audio, but in order for them to remember the pronunciation, tell them to mark the stress as they listen. Later when they practice on their own, they will be able to pronounce the words correctly.

Strategy

Getting Meaning from Context

- On the board, put the phrase *Clues to Meaning*. Under it, write the following words:
  1. *for example, for instance such as among them* > introduce examples
  2. opposite meaning of a new word
  3. *that is in other words* > introduce a definition or explanation
- Call on different students to read each clue and example in the box.
- Tell students to look for these new clues to meaning when they see words or phrases they don't understand. These clues to meaning will help them understand new words and phrases.

4 Getting Meaning from Context

- Read the directions and the first example.
- Have students complete the activity individually.

ANSWER KEY

1. predict = say in advance that something will happen developing countries = India and Nigeria
2. gridlock = traffic that doesn't move commute = go from home to work and back
3. affluent = rich
4. priorities = list of what was most important
5. trash = garbage
6. produce = fruits and vegetables (oranges or potatoes)
7. recycling plant = factory or place where glass bottles, plastic, and cans are made into new products
8. mass-transit = a system of transportation for many people
9. agricultural operation = farm crops = plants that produce food (grain, fruit, vegetables)
10. cultivate = grow
11. urban dwellers = city people

Read

5 Reading an Article

- Write *"What is the city Curitiba, Brazil, doing right?"* on the board and ask students to think about this question as they are reading.
- Have the students read the passage silently within a time limit (10–15 minutes), or have them follow along as you play the audio.
- Tell them to underline any words or phrases that are new or that they don't understand. Remind them **not** to use a dictionary during this part of the lesson.
- Tell students to look at activity **6 Recognizing the Main Idea** if they finish the reading.
- Start the audio.

After You Read

FOCUS

Identifying the Main Idea

- Call on a student to read the information in the box to remind them about the main idea.

6 Identifying the Main Idea

- Read the directions and give the students a few minutes to find the main idea in Paragraphs B and G.
- Tell students who have already completed the activity to check their answers with a partner.
- Go around the room and check to see if students have found the answers.
- Call on two students to read their answers. Ask if the other students agree. Confirm the answers.

ANSWER KEY

From Paragraph B: The city of Curitiba, Brazil, proves that it's possible for even a city in a developing country to offer a good life to its residents.

From Paragraph G: Curitiba is truly, as Lewis Mumford once said of cities in general, a "symbol of the possible."

Strategy

Identifying Supporting Details

- Read this paragraph to the class or call on a student to read it.
- On the board, draw a large box on the left side and several smaller ones on the right side. Connect them with lines like the ones on page 30.
- Write *Main Idea* in the large box and *Details* in each of the smaller ones.
- Tell the students that this type of graphic organizer will help them to understand a reading passage better.

Best Practice

Organizing Information

Activities such as Activity 7 will teach students to organize information from a reading passage using a graphic organizer. This activity allows students to locate the information so that they can better recall it at a later date. In this case, they record the supporting details from three paragraphs in the reading passage.

7 Identifying Supporting Details

- Read the directions.
- Read the words in the first box on the left and the first box on the right.
- Tell the students they have to find three more details about "*Green Exchange*" and write them in the other three boxes.
- Check the answers together before they do the next set of boxes.
- Put students in pairs and tell them to fill in the remaining boxes about Paragraphs D and E with a partner.
- Give them a time limit of 10–15 minutes.
- Go around the room and check students' answers.
- When most of the students have finished, check the answers.

ANSWER KEY

Wording of answers may vary.

C. cleans the streets of trash / exchanges trash for fresh produce / recycles two-thirds of garbage / gives jobs to poor people

D. decreases traffic / makes commuting more pleasant / helps solve problem of air pollution

E. gives poor people jobs / helps them turn their lives around

counseling
medical care
job training

FOCUS

Understanding Italics

- Print a word on the board in straight letters, for example, huge. Then print it in slanted letters, for example, *huge*.
- Tell students that italics mean that the letters are slanted or leaning to one side.
- Read the sentences in the box or have two students read them.
- Tell them that they are going to look for italics in the reading passage.

8 Understanding Italics

- Read the directions.
- Tell students to work quickly.
- When they have finished, ask them to count the number of words or phrases they circled (5) and the number of words/phrases they underlined (3).
- Elicit the words from the class, one by one.

ANSWER KEY

Paragraph A	*some*	emphasis
Paragraph B	*aren't*	emphasis
Paragraph C	*Cambio Verde* *two-thirds*	foreign emphasis
Paragraph D	*decreased* *before*	emphasis emphasis
Paragraph E	*Fazenda da Solidaridade* *Verde Saude*	foreign foreign

FOCUS

Understanding Contrast

- Call on a student to read the information in the Box.

9 Understanding Contrast

- Read the directions.
- Ask students to look back at the reading.
- Give them a few minutes to find the contrast and decide where it can be divided (between Paragraphs B and C). Paragraphs A and B describe the problems; the remaining paragraphs describe some of the solutions.
- Ask a student to read the last sentence of paragraph B and tell what the contrasting words are (problems/solutions).

Strategy

Critical Thinking: Making Inferences

- Read the directions.
- Write these sentences on the board:

  The average income in Curitiba was only $2,000 per year.
  Many people didn't have enough money to live well.
- Point out that in the first sentence, the information is clearly stated. In the second sentence, the idea is implied, but not clearly stated.
- Tell the students they will look back at the reading to do the next activity.

10 Making Inferences

- Read the directions.
- Give students a time limit to do the activity (10–15 minutes).
- Check the answers when they have finished.

ANSWER KEY

1. S **2.** I **3.** S **4.** S **5.** S **6.** S
7. I **8.** S

11 Discussing the Reading

- Divide students into small groups from different countries or regions, if possible.
- Have them discuss the questions in this section. They may not know some of the answers.
- When they finish, do the Expansion Activity below.

Best Practice

Interacting with Others
Activities such as this will encourage the students to work together to complete a project. Since there are several different areas of research, students can work individually and then share their findings with the group, enlarging their scope of learning.

REPRODUCIBLE

Expansion Activity

- The aim of this activity is for students to do collaborative research on the topics from the discussion of the reading. They will share this information with their group and then each group will share it with the class.
- Photocopy and distribute **Black Line Master 4** "Major Cities" on page BLM4 of this Teacher's Manual.
- Tell students to choose a country and complete the sheet, looking up information on the Internet.
- When they have finished, ask them to share their findings with the class.

Sick-Building Syndrome

Before You Read

1 Making Predictions

- Ask students if they ever see any pollution outside.
- Then ask them if there is any pollution inside buildings, like houses, schools, malls, or other places.
- Tell them to look at pages 32–33, read the directions and look at the chart.
- Divide them into small groups and have them complete the chart.
- When they finish, elicit answers and write them on the board.

ANSWER KEY

Answers may vary.

Causes of Outdoor Air Pollution	Causes of Indoor Air Pollution
— *motorcycles, cars, buses, trucks, trains, ships* — *factories, industrial complexes* — *plants that produce electricity, natural gas, petroleum, or nuclear power*	— *smoking cigarettes, cigars, pipes* — *fires for cooking or heating, stoves* — *chemicals in household cleaners, paint, varnish, carpets, insulation, or other synthetic materials*

Read

2 Skimming for Main Ideas

- Read the directions.
- Have the students read the passage silently within a time limit (10–15 minutes), or have them follow along as you play the audio.
- After each paragraph, stop the audio and have the students write the topic and main idea of the paragraph.
- As an alternative, have them underline the topic and main idea as they're listening, and when the passage is finished, have them discuss their answers with a small group before they write them.
- Remind them **not** to use a dictionary during this part of the lesson.
- Start the audio.
- When the passage is finished, check the answers with the class.

ANSWER KEY

Answers may vary.

A. Topic: Sick-building syndrome
Main Idea: Some buildings create their own indoor air pollution.

B. Topic: Indoor air pollution
Main Idea: The air inside some buildings is full of pollutants…

✓**C.** Topic: Types of indoor air pollution
Main Idea: Many products give off chemicals we can't see but breathe in.

D. Topic: How indoor air becomes polluted
Main Idea: Some products release chemicals into the air and lack of ventilation makes the situation more serious.

E. Topic: Solutions to sick-building syndrome
Main Idea: Experts must determine the cause and workers must remove it.

F. Topic: Plants as a solution
Main Idea: Some plants remove pollutants from the air.

G. Topic: More research is necessary
Main Idea: Plants may offer an important pollution-control system for 21st century.

After You Read

Best Practice

Cultivating Critical Thinking
Activities such as comparing answers with a partner encourage students to listen to and learn from others. By not depending completely on the teacher to supply all the answers, students become more independent and learn to engage in critical thinking.

3 Checking Your Answers

- When the passage is finished, put students into pairs or small groups to check their answers from Activity 2.
- Go around and answer questions and check answers.
- If there is time, students can go to the board and write the **Topic** and **Main Idea** so the class can check all together.

4 Understanding Pronoun Reference

- Read the directions.
- Tell students to continue working in small groups to find the referents to the pronouns.
- When they are finished, check the answers.

ANSWER KEY

1. teachers and students **2.** people
3. chemicals **4.** sources **5.** solutions
6. workers **7.** plants

Strategy

Scanning
- Read the information in the box.
- Have a volunteer demonstrate the steps using a paragraph from "Sick-Building Syndrome."

5 Scanning

- Read the directions and the questions.
- When students have finished scanning, go over the answers together.

6 Discussing the Reading

- Read the directions.
- Tell students to continue working in small groups to discuss the answers to the questions.
- Ask students to share answers with the class.

Responding in Writing

7 Summarizing

- Remind students of the lesson on Summarizing from Chapter 1. Ask them these questions:

  What do summaries contain? (main idea and important details)

  Should they be copied from the paragraph? (No, they should be in writer's own words.)

  Should they be as long as the original paragraph? (No, they should be shorter.)
- Read the directions.
- Divide the class into 3 sections. Assign one of the paragraphs (C, D, or E) from Part 1 on page 28 to each section.
- Have students read their paragraph again, and then tell them to look at the graphic organizer on pages 30–31 where the main idea and important details have already been written.
- Tell them to write the summary from the graphic organizer.
- Go around the room and check the students' work.
- If they finish early, they can read the summary of another student in the same section.
- If there is time, ask one student from each section to write his or her summary on the board and go over them with the class.

8 Writing Your Own Ideas

Best Practice

Scaffolding Instruction

Activities such as writing about their thoughts enable students to be more successful when they work independently. This activity uses the students' prior knowledge of the reading as a scaffold. With the teachers' guidance, the students are able to contribute to the summary on the board. Then they are better equipped to write a summary by themselves.

- Tell students to choose one of the topics for homework.
- In class have the students think about and write the main idea of their paragraph and then complete the paragraph at home.

Talk it Over

9 Interviewing

- You may want to use the **Black Line Master** described here to conduct this activity.
- Alternatively, have students create their own interview sheets and follow the instructions provided for the BLM.

REPRODUCIBLE

Expansion Activity

- The aim of this activity is for students to gather opinions and predictions from others while interacting in English. They will share this information with the class when they are finished.
- Photocopy and distribute **Black Line Master 5** "City Life In The Future" on page BLM5 of this Teacher's Manual.
- Model the activity. Call on a student and say *"Hello. My name is… , and I'm interviewing people for a class assignment. Can you tell me your opinion about city life? Will it be better or worse than it is today? Can you tell me two reasons why? Can you make predictions about how city life will be different in the future?*
- Point out that they should conduct these interviews in English, if possible. They should also write the person's answers on the paper.
- Give students a few days to complete this assignment.
- When it is finished, elicit answers from students in a large group format. Write some of the reasons and predictions on the board.

1 Focusing on Words from the Academic Word List

- Read the directions.
- Give students a time limit (10–15 minutes).
- Tell students to check their answers with a partner if they finish quickly.
- Ask how many got all correct, one wrong, two wrong, and so on.

ANSWER KEY

1. predict 2. global 3. transportation
4. access 5. residents 6. established
7. priorities 8. focus 9. environment

Culture

Language Similarities: False Cognates

- Read the Culture box together.
- Have students give cognates and false cognates in their language.

Strategy

Understanding Parts of Speech

- Write the sentence from the **Example** on the board along with the following sentence and point out the parts of speech:

noun
Cities around the globe need to find solutions to similar problems, so city
adjective
planners sometimes meet at a global conference. They discuss issues that
adverb
affect them globally.

- Then tell the students to look at page 40. Read the directions in the box.
- Ask a student to read the sentences on the board. Explain the parts of speech in the sentences.

2 Understanding Parts of Speech

- Tell the students to look at the chart in the following section. Read the directions.
- After the students have completed the chart, play the audio as students check their answers.

ANSWER KEY

1. beautiful	5. difficulty	9. safe
2. create	6. efficiently	10. solution
3. crowd	7. polluted	11. worse
4. differ	8. prediction	

- Read the directions of the next section. Students can work individually or in pairs.

ANSWER KEY

1. solution (n) / solve (v)
2. pollution (n) / pollutants (n)
3. crowds (n) / crowded (adj)
4. safe (adj) / safely (adv) / safety (n)
5. beautiful (adj) / beautify (v)
6. predict (v) / worse (adj) / predictions (n) / worsen (v)
7. differ (v) / difference (n) / differently (adv) / different (adj)
8. efficient (adj) / efficiently (adv)

FOCUS

Looking up Parts of Speech

- Read the directions.
- On the board, write a few prepositions (by, at, in) and conjunctions (and, but, or) so that students know what they are.
- Write these sentences on the board and elicit the parts of speech for the underlined words from the students:

noun
A: The <u>reason</u> he was late is that the subway wasn't running.

verb *conjunction* *adverb*
So he <u>had to walk</u> to class, <u>but</u> he walked as <u>quickly</u> as possible.

adjective
B: That sounds <u>reasonable</u>. It's about a mile from his

preposition
house <u>to</u> the university.

3 Looking Up Parts of Speech

- Tell the students that this activity will be a contest.
- Instruct them to look up the words in their dictionaries. If students have both electronic and paperback dictionaries, divide them into two groups. The students who finish first in each group are the winners.
- Check the answers of the winners to make sure they put both possible parts of speech for answers 2, 3, 4, 6, 8, 9, 11, 14, and 15.
- Have them read their answers to the class.

ANSWER KEY

1. adj **2.** n/v **3.** n/v **4.** n/adj **5.** adj
6. n/v **7.** n **8.** n/v **9.** n/v **10.** n **11.** n/v
12. adv **13.** n **14.** n/adj **15.** n/v

4 Searching the Internet

Best Practice

Making Use of Academic Content
Activities such as this prepare the students for academic research. By looking up articles in online newspapers and taking notes on main ideas and details, they will become more familiar with the process of note-taking from primary sources and better prepared for academic work.

- Take the students to the computer lab or have them go after class to do this assignment with **Black Line Master 6**.

REPRODUCIBLE

Expansion Activity

- The aim of this activity is for students to find an online newspaper in English from a different country and read an article. They will look up this information with a partner and then share their article with the class.
- Photocopy and distribute **Black Line Master 6** "English–Language Newspapers" on page BLM6 of this Teacher's Manual.
- Have the students work in pairs and let them choose (or assign them) a country.
- They can use Google or <u>www.onlinenewspapers.com</u> to find a newspaper.
- Tell students to find an article about the capital city and write some main ideas and details from the article.
- Give students a few days to complete this assignment.
- When it is finished, ask students to report their findings to the class.

FOCUS TOEFL® iBT

Getting Meaning of Vocabulary from Context

- Write these terms on the board:

  Close in meaning correct—not correct

  Correct part of speech—wrong meaning

  Wrong answer

  Wrong part of speech
- Read or explain the information in the box to the students and refer to the terms on the board.

1 Practice

- Read the directions and have the students complete the activity.
- As you check the answers, ask students why the other answers are not correct. Refer to the terms on board.

ANSWER KEY

1. C/B **2.** D **3.** C **4.** D

Self-Assessment Log

- Read the directions aloud and have students check vocabulary they learned in the chapter and are prepared to use.
- Have students check the strategies practiced in the chapter (or the degree to which they learned them). They have actually used all these strategies in Chapter 2.
- Put students in small groups. Ask students to find the information or an activity related to each strategy in the group.
- Tell students to find definitions in the chapter for any words they did not check.

Best Practice

Activating Prior Knowledge

Activities such as this, help students make text-to-text connections. They have previewed the vocabulary, read it in the passage, and practiced it in the activities. Doing a dictation will help the students to use the words in a slightly different context and test their knowledge. It will also allow the teacher to see if the students have actually learned the words from the chapter and incorporated them into their lexicon.

Expansion Activity

- The aim of this activity is for students to practice writing words from the reading passage in this chapter in sentences.
- Tell the students to study the vocabulary for a few minutes for a dictation.
- Have them take out a piece of paper.
- Dictate these sentences to them. The underlined words are from the list:
  1. <u>Urban dwellers</u> in <u>developing countries</u> have to <u>solve</u> many <u>environmental</u> problems.
  2. Often, their leaders do not have <u>access</u> to a lot of money, so they have to be <u>creative</u> and make a list of <u>priorities</u>.
  3. When they <u>establish</u> which problems they will work on, they <u>focus</u> on them and develop <u>efficient methods</u> for <u>solving</u> them.
  4. Generally, they involve <u>mass transit, trash recycling, crowded</u> living, and <u>agricultural operations</u>.
  5. Although the cities are not <u>affluent</u>, some leaders <u>produce</u> results by <u>predicting</u> that with the help of the public, these problems can be <u>solved</u>.
- When the students have finished, collect the papers and check them.
- For variety, have them write the sentences on the board and check their own papers.

CHAPTER 3

Business and Money

In this CHAPTER

Students will read about different aspects of business and money, from people who cannot afford to buy anything to people who buy too much. In the first reading, they will learn about microlending and two important leaders in this movement: Mohammad Yunus from Bangladesh and Anne Firth Murray from the United States. Both these leaders saw that the only way to eradicate poverty was to give the poor a chance to support themselves through small businesses and to develop solutions to their own problems. In the second reading, students will learn about the psychology of consumerism, or the way advertisers convince us to buy things we don't need. By targeting our dissatisfaction or fear, marketing experts are better able to sell us products that may be unnecessary or even dangerous.

> "Prosperity is a way of living and thinking, and not just money or things. Poverty is a way of living and thinking, and not just a lack of money or things."
>
> Eric Butterworth
> Scholar, author of *Spiritual Economics* (1916–2003)

Chapter Opener

- Direct students' attention to the photo. Then have students work in small groups to answer the questions in the Connecting to the Topic box. Go over the answers as a class.
- Read the quotation by Butterworth and ask students what it means.
- Put two words on the board: *Prosperity* and *Poverty*
- Put students in pairs to find several words or phrases to put under each word.
- Call on students to share their words or phrases with the class.
- Check students' comprehension of the words: *Prosperity* and *Poverty*.

Chapter Overview

Reading Selections
Banking on Poor Women
Consumerism and the Human Brain

Reading Skills and Strategies
Previewing the topic and vocabulary
Identifying the main idea and details
Understanding conclusions
Skimming for the topic and the main ideas
Paying attention to phrases

Critical-Thinking Skills
Identifying problems and solutions
Organizing ideas using a Venn diagram
Comparing and contrasting
Making inferences
Understanding irony
Analyzing advertisements
Summarizing a paragraph

Vocabulary Building
Getting meaning from context (*e.g.* and *i.e.*)
Using parts of speech to understand vocabulary
Using suffixes to identify parts of speech
Recognizing synonyms
Focusing on the Academic Word List

Language Skills
Understanding pronoun reference
Discussing social problems and solutions
Analyzing advertisements
Writing a paragraph

Focus on Testing TOEFL® iBT
Focusing on implications and inferences

Vocabulary

Nouns
- access*
- capacity*
- character
- collateral
- common knowledge
- consumer*
- economy*
- eradication
- fund*
- grants*
- items*
- microlending
- poverty
- requirement*

Verbs
- consume*
- invest*
- target*

Adjectives
- anonymous
- identical*
- social
- subsidiary*
- worthless

Expressions
- peer pressure
- took (take) the initiative

*These words are from the Academic Word List. For more information on this list, see www.victoria.ac.nz/lals/resources/ academicwordlist/.

Banking on Poor Women

Before You Read

1 Previewing the Topic

- Put students in small groups and have them look at the photos.
- Have students read the questions on pages 48–49 and discuss the answers.
- Call on students to share their answers with the class.
- Write some of the problems and solutions on the board and discuss them with the class.

2 Thinking Ahead

- Read the quotations to the students.
- Ask the students to restate them and write a restatement on the board for each one.
- Ask the class which ones they agree or disagree with and why.

3 Previewing Vocabulary

- Read the directions to the students.
- Have them put a check (✓) next to the words they know.
- Tell them to put the stress on words of more than one syllable as they listen to the audio.
- Write these words on the board as examples: *capa'city, pov'erty, anon'ymous.*
- Remind them **not** to use a dictionary during this part of the lesson.
- Start the audio.

ANSWER KEY

Nouns
ac'cess
capac'ity
char'acter
collat'eral
eradica'tion
fund
grants
lit'eracy
microlend'ing
pov'erty
require'ment

Verbs
fund'ing
invest'
lift

Adjectives
anon'ymous
so'cial
subsid'iary
worth'less

Expressions
peer' pressure
took (take) the ini'tiative

Strategy

Getting Meaning from Context: Understanding *e.g.* and *i.e.*

- On the board, put the phrase *Clues to Meaning.* Under it, write the following abbreviations and examples:

  1. *e.g. = for example*
  2. *i.e. = that is; in other words*

- *She traveled through several countries in Latin America—e.g., Argentina, Bolivia, and Chile.*
- *She worked as a photojournalist; i.e., she took pictures and wrote stories about the people she met.*
- Tell students to look for these new clues to meaning when they see words or phrases they don't understand. These clues will help them understand new words and phrases.

4 Getting Meaning from Context

- Read the directions and have students work on the activity individually.

ANSWER KEY

1. entrepreneurs = people who own and run their own small businesses
2. peer pressure = group members make sure that each person pays back his or her loan
3. social ills = violence and lack of health care and education

Strategy

Recognizing Similar Meanings but Different Parts of Speech

- Write the example on the board.
- Above **poverty**, write *noun*, and above **poor**, write *adjective*.
- Read the explanation to the students.
- Write another example on the board: *There may be **social** ills when many people in a **society** have no money to buy necessities.*
- Above **social**, write *adjective*, and above **society**, write *noun*.
- Repeat the explanation to the students.

5 Recognizing Synonyms

- Read the directions.
- Ask a student to read the sentence.
- Call on different students to give the answers.

ANSWER KEY

1. n **2.** is honest **3.** n **4.** is able to run her business

Strategy

Using Parts of Speech to Understand Vocabulary

- Write the example sentence in the **Strategy Box** on the board.
- Read the first part of the explanation to the students.
- Ask them what part of speech **approve** is and write *verb* above it.
- Ask them what they think it means and write their answers on the board (*agree, say OK about, sign*).
- Read the last part of the explanation.

6 Using Parts of Speech to Understand Vocabulary

- Read the directions.
- Remind students **not** to use a dictionary during this part of the lesson.
- Go around the room and help students if necessary.

ANSWER KEY

Answers may vary.

1.	lift	v.	bring, carry
2.	eradication	n.	elimination, removal
3.	subsidiary	adj.	side, minor
4.	fund	n.	account, group, money
	grant	n.	not loans, money given
5.	invest	v.	put in

Read

7 Reading an Article

- Write *"How can banks help poor women to change their lives?"* on the board and ask students to think about this question as they are reading.

- Have the students read the passage silently within a time limit (10–15 minutes), or have them follow along as you play the audio.
- Tell them to underline any words or phrases that are new or that they don't understand.
- Remind them **not** to use a dictionary during this part of the lesson.
- Start the audio.

After You Read

Strategy

Organizing Ideas: Focusing on Using a Venn Diagram

- Tell students to look at the **Strategy Box**.
- Read the explanation to the students.
- Draw a set of circles on the board (a Venn diagram). Draw a simple car and a motorcycle in the circles.
- Elicit similarities from the students and write the words in the center. Use prompts such as *They both have/are...* Students may give answers like *transportation, wheels, seats, engine, gas, fast*, and so on.
- Elicit the differences and write the words on the right or left. Students may give answers like *large, 4 wheels, big engine, 4 seats, expensive* for the car, and *small, 2 wheels, small engine, 2 seats, cheap* for the motorcycle.
- Tell the students that a Venn diagram is a graphic organizer that they can use when they read. It will help them remember similarities and differences between two or more concepts in a reading.
- Now look at the Venn diagram with the oranges and bananas.
- Ask a student to read the words in the center. Ask other students to read the words on the right and left.
- Left (yellow color, long, curved shape); right (orange color, round shape).
- Ask the students what the two fruits have in common. The students should give you the answers from the center of the Venn diagram—(fruit, sweet).

REPRODUCIBLE Expansion Activity

- The aim of this activity is for students to practice using Venn diagrams to differentiate between two categories. They will choose two sets of things and figure out similarities and differences. Then they will share their answers with a partner.
- Photocopy and distribute **Black Line Master 7** "Venn Diagrams" on page BLM7 of this Teacher's Manual.
- Write a few suggestions on the board: *two people in your family, two cities, two sports, two majors, two types of food*, and so on. Tell them to label their diagrams. Remind them they need to complete two sets of Venn diagrams.
- Have the students work individually at first. When they finish, tell them to share their diagrams with a partner. Then tell them to switch and share their diagrams with another partner.

8 Organizing Ideas Using a Venn Diagram

- Read the directions.
- Give the students a few minutes to find the similarities and differences between the **Grameen Bank** and the **Global Fund for Women**.
- Go around the room and check to see if students have found the answers.
- Have the students check their work with a partner if they finish early.
- Draw two intersecting circles on the board (a Venn diagram) and ask three students to go to the board. One will write the similarities and the other two will write the differences.

- When they finish, ask if the other students agree. Discuss the answers.

ANSWER KEY

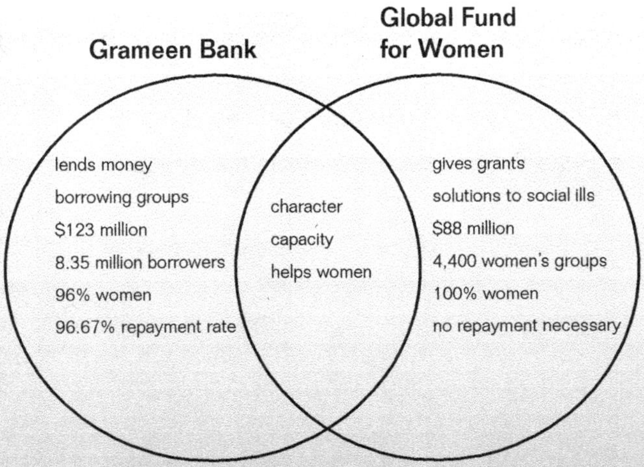

❾ Checking Comprehension: Identifying Details

Best Practice

Interacting with Others

Activities such as this will encourage the students to work together to find answers to questions. Since they cannot look back at the reading, they will have to depend on the knowledge and understanding of the members of their group. This will encourage them to engage in peer interaction and collaboration.

- You may want to put students in small groups.
- Have them answer the questions together, with each group writing its answers on one piece of paper.
- Tell them they can use the Venn diagram or ask others in their group, but they can't look back at the reading for the answers.
- Ask them to share their answers with the class.

ANSWER KEY

Answers may vary.

1. To borrow money from Grameen Bank, women must have character and capacity and join a borrowing group. It isn't necessary to have collateral.
2. The bank lends to women because men usually spend money on themselves, but women spend money on the business. It doesn't lend to people in urban areas because borrowers in cities do not always repay the loans. Because of peer pressure, microlending is more effective in small villages, where everyone knows everyone else.
3. While the primary effect is the eradication of poverty, the subsidiary effect is the change in the social status of women. They receive more respect because they have more money and more capacity for business.
4. Some of the social ills associated with poverty are violence against women, lack of health care, and lack of education.

❿ Critical Thinking: Making Inferences

- Read the directions to the students.
- Ask a student to read the information from paragraph E.
- Elicit ways in which the students think a "woman receives more respect."
- Write some of them on the board. Students may say:

  Her husband is kind to her.
  He helps her with the business.
  Her neighbors buy things from her.
  Her children help her at home.
  She buys things that her family needs.
  The people at the bank welcome her.
  She sends her children to school.
  The teachers talk to her about her children.
  The villagers talk to her about her business.
  She feels more important at home and in the village.

- Write the word **Inferences** above the list.
- Tell students that although these sentences are actually not in the reading, we can **infer** them from the reading.

11 Discussing the Reading

- Read the directions to the students.
- Put students in small groups.
- Have them talk about the answers.
- Ask them to share their answers with the class.

ANSWER KEY

(Answers will vary.)

1. Some banks require collateral like a car, a house, and a steady job. They may require a credit history, proving you have paid back loans in the past.
2. They may join a credit union, which is like a bank, but the interest is usually lower.
3. There might be crime, poverty, pollution, unemployment, corrupt politicians, and so forth. Political parties or other groups sometimes try to solve these problems.

12 Talk It Over: Understanding Irony

- Direct the students' attention to the cartoon.
- Have two students read the parts of the rich man and poor man.
- Ask them what they think the cartoon is expressing and if they agree with it.
- They may have different opinions about it.
- Read the definition of *irony* in the direction line.

Consumerism and the Human Brain

Before You Read

Strategy

Previewing the Topic

- Read the explanation to the students.

1 Previewing the Topic

- Read the directions to the students.
- Put the students in small groups.
- Tell them to answer the questions.
- Have them share their answers with the class.

Read

2 Identifying the Topic and Main Idea

- Read the directions.
- Have the students read the passage silently within a time limit (10–15 minutes), or have them follow along as you play the audio.
- After each paragraph, stop the audio and have the students write the topic and main idea of the paragraph.
- Or have them underline the topic and main idea as they're listening, and when the passage is finished, have them discuss their answers with a small group before they write them.
- Remind them **not** to use a dictionary during this part of the lesson.
- Start the audio.

ANSWER KEY

Answers may vary.

A. Topic: Consumerism
Main Idea: We buy products based on marketers' successful use of psychology.

B. Topic: Human fears
Main Idea: Our fear of offending people is greater than logic.

C. Topic: Need for good self-image
Main Idea: Our need for a good self-image leads us to irrational decisions about products.

D. Topic: Identical products
Main Idea: Even though products are the same, people choose one based on sensory information.

E. Topic: Self-fulfilling prophecy
Main Idea: When we buy products, we believe what advertisers say about them, and it comes true.

F. Topic: Making choices
Main Idea: We may not make choices independently; marketers may make them for us.

After You Read

3 Identifying the Topic and Main Idea

- Read the directions.
- Put students in pairs.
- Go around the room and answer questions.

4 Understanding Pronoun Reference

- Read the directions to the students.

ANSWER KEY

1. marketers **2.** dentists **3.** men
4. a product **5.** Dr. Alan Hirsch **6.** consumers

Content Note

- In the United States, there are several organizations that monitor the value and safety of products and evaluate the claims advertisers make about them. They also act as advocates for consumers and defend their rights. Two of these organizations are discussed below.
- The **Consumers Union** was an organization founded in 1936 with the mission of protecting consumers from the false claims of advertisers and the dangers of unsafe products. It began publishing a magazine that is now called **Consumer Reports**, which is still published today. There is also a website of the same name that gives ratings and recommendations on the following categories of products: cars, appliances, electronics and computers, home and garden, health and fitness, personal finance, babies and kids, travel, and food. Millions of people subscribe to the magazine or website to get the latest information on consumer products.
- **California Certified Organic Farmers** (CCOF) is an organization founded in 1973 to help farmers who wanted to use organic (not synthetic) products to produce food. This included fertilizers and pesticides for plants and food and medicine for animals. Today, the CCOF label is recognized and trusted by people who buy organic meat, vegetables, fruit, and packaged food. Products cannot be labeled "Certified Organic" unless they pass inspection by CCOF. Other organizations, like the **Organic Consumers Association**, monitor local and national regulations on the production and labeling and of food and personal products.

Best Practice

Making Use of Academic Content
Activities such as this Expansion Activity prepare the students for real-world academic research. By looking up websites of different organizations and taking notes on facts and figures, they will become more familiar with the process and better prepared for academic work.

REPRODUCIBLE

Expansion Activity

- The aim of this activity is for students to do collaborative research on a topic from the reading. They will share this information with their group, and then each group will share it with the class.
- Photocopy and distribute **Black Line Master 8** "Consumer Organizations In My Country" on page BLM8 of this Teacher's Manual.
- Tell students to complete the sheet in pairs, looking up information on the Internet. Make sure each pair chooses a different organization to research.
- When they have finished, ask them to share their findings with the class.

5 Discussing the Reading

- Read the directions.
- Have students do Steps 1 and 2 individually.
- When they finish, divide them into groups of males and females to share their lists and answers for Step 3.
- When they finish, have a class discussion about the answers.
- Ask students if they noticed any differences in the answers given by males and females.
- If there are differences, draw a Venn diagram on the board with two circles and elicit the similarities and differences, writing them on the board.

Responding in Writing

6 Summarizing

- Read the directions.
- Remind students of the lesson on Summarizing from Chapter 1. Ask them these questions:

  What do summaries contain? (Topic, Main idea and important details.)

  Should they be copied from the paragraph? (No, they should be in writer's own words.)

  Should they be as long as the original paragraph? (No, they should be shorter.)
- Assign students to a paragraph or let them choose one.
- Tell students to sit in small groups and compose a summary together, with each student writing on a separate paper.
- Have a student from each group write his or her paragraph on the board. Correct any errors.

7 Responding in Writing

- Assign the paragraph in this section for homework, allowing each student to choose a topic.
- Tell students to write the main idea on the last line in the directions for this activity.
- When students bring their homework in, before you collect it, tell them to exchange papers and read their partner's paragraph.
- Ask them to write the main idea of the paragraph they have just read under the paragraph.
- When students get their papers back, have them compare their main idea with the one their partners wrote.
- Collect the papers and correct.

Talk It Over

8 Discussing Advertisements

Best Practice

Cultivating Critical Thinking

Activities such as collaboratively analyzing advertisements encourage students to look at the media more critically. By discussing ads, answering questions, and writing about them, students can become more sophisticated consumers as they analyze the psychology used in advertising.

- Go over the directions with students.
- Have students create a chart with the questions and answers for each ad.

Reproducible — Expansion Activity

- The aim of this activity is for students to do collaborative research on a topic from the reading. They will share this information with their group and then each group will share it with the class.
- Photocopy and distribute **Black Line Master 9** "Analyzing Advertisements" on page BLM9 of this Teacher's Manual.
- Let each group choose a different product and find several advertisements.
- Tell students to answer the questions about their advertisement and write a short paragraph about what kind of psychology the advertisers are using.
- When they have finished, have them share their findings with the class.

1 Recognizing Word Meanings

- Read the directions.
- Have students do the activity quickly without using a dictionary.

ANSWER KEY

1. d **2.** a **3.** b **4.** e **5.** c

2 Focusing on Words from the Academic Word List

- Read the directions.
- Have students do the activity quickly without using a dictionary.
- For variety, play the audio (first two paragraphs) and do the activity as a dictation.
- Have students check the answers on page 58 of the Student Book.

ANSWER KEY

1. consumers	**6.** identical
2. consume	**7.** consume
3. economy	**8.** targeting
4. access	**9.** logic
5. items	

FOCUS

Understanding Parts of Speech: Suffixes

- Read the paragraph to the class or call on a student to read it.
- On the board, write *Nouns* on the left side and *Adjectives* on the right side.
- Write *actor*, *artist*, and *presentation* under *Nouns*.
- Elicit the adjective form of these words (*active*, *artistic*, and *presentable*) and write them under *Adjectives*.
- Underline the suffixes.
- Tell students that recognizing suffixes will help them identify parts of speech, which will help them figure out the meaning of new words.

3 Understanding Parts of Speech: Suffixes

- Read the directions.
- Have students do the activity.
- Check the answers.

ANSWER KEY

1. adj	**12.** adj	**23.** n
2. n	**13.** n	**24.** adj
3. adj	**14.** n	**25.** n
4. n	**15.** n	**26.** adj
5. n	**16.** n	**27.** n
6. n	**17.** n	**28.** adj
7. adj	**18.** n	**29.** n
8. adj	**19.** adj	**30.** n/adj
9. n	**20.** adj	**31.** adj
10. n	**21.** n	**32.** adj
11. adj	**22.** n	**33.** n

4 Understanding Parts of Speech: Changing the Suffix

- Read the directions.
- Have students do the activity.
- Check the answers.

ANSWER KEY

1. Marketers/consumers
2. violent/offensive
3. information/influence
4. successful/society

Strategy

Paying Attention to Phrases

- Write the phrases in the **Strategy Box** on the board, marking the stress.
- Read the directions.
- Have students repeat the phrases after you.
- Have them repeat them by themselves.

Noun Phrases

greater ac'cess
access to infor'mation

Verb Phrases

spend mon'ey
educate peo'ple
to spend wise'ly

Prepositional Phrases

in a sim'ilar way
with exciting lives'

Infinitive Phrases

to save mon'ey
to buy Brand X'

5 Paying Attention to Phrases

- Read the directions.
- Have students take turns reading one sentence each, saying what kind of phrase it is.
- Then say the phrases and have the students repeat them after you.

ANSWER KEY

1. prep. **2.** noun **3.** prep.
For many people, there seems to be no *escape from poverty*; *in other words*, they are poor, and they
4. verb **5.** prep. **6.** noun
have no hope that this will ever change. *In addition*, they have the *social problems* of poverty.
7. verb **8.** noun **9.** verb **10.** prep.
Imagine this situation: *a poor woman* *has an idea* for a *small business* to lift herself and her family
11. prep. **12.** noun **13.** inf. **14.** verb **15.** inf.
out of poverty. She needs *a little money* *to begin this business*. She *goes* *to a bank* *to borrow the money*,
16. prep. **17.** verb
and the banker interviews her. At this bank, as *at most banks*, the borrower must *meet three necessary*
18. inf. **19.** prep.
conditions: character, capacity, and collateral. That is, if this woman wants *to borrow money* *from the bank*,
20. verb **21.** inf.
she must show that she (1) is honest (*has character*), (2) is able *to run her business* (has capacity), and
22. verb
(3) *owns a house*, land, or something valuable (has collateral) for the bank to take if she can't
23. verb **24.** verb
pay back the money. So what happens to the woman? The bank won't *lend her the money* because she
25. prep.
doesn't have any collateral. *In such a situation*, there seems to be no way for the woman
26. inf.
to break the cycle of poverty.

6 Noticing Words in Phrases

- Read the directions.
- Have students do the activity individually. Tell them to try to do it *before* reading the paragraphs.
- Tell students to check the answers themselves by reading the paragraphs.

ANSWER KEY

A. **1.** to **2.** with **3.** to **4.** dental **5.** dental **6.** of

B. **7.** in **8.** take/of **9.** common **10.** to **11.** of

C. **12.** utility **13.** up **14.** out of

7 Searching the Internet

Best Practice

Organizing Information

Activities such as this will teach students to organize information from a Web page using a graphic organizer. This activity allows students to locate information so that they can better recall it at a later date. In this case, they look up the information on the Internet and take notes as they read.

ANSWER KEY

Organization	Question	Answer (Answers may vary.)
Grameen Bank	What types of businesses do Grameen borrowers have?	Making shoes, dairy products; selling clothing, food, plants, produce, etc.
Global Fund for Women	What is one program that the Global Fund is currently supporting?	Increasing access to education, fostering social change, expanding civic and political participation, etc.
Seikatsu Club	What are some of the club's principles on safety, health, and the environment?	Pursuit of safety for consumer materials, reduction of harmful substances, sustainable use of natural resources, etc.

FOCUS TOEFL® iBT

Implications and Inferences

- Write these terms on the board:

  Imply – communicate indirectly (not directly)
  - "I implied that..."
  - "The author implies that..."
  - "Paragraph 4 implies that..."

  Infer – understand indirectly (not directly)
  - "I inferred that..."
  - "Readers might infer that..."
  - "The police inferred that..."
- Read or explain the instructions to the students and refer to the terms on the board.

1 Practice

- Have students do the activity.
- As you check the answers, ask students why some of the answers are not correct. Refer to the terms on board.

ANSWER KEY

1. ✓ **2.** *infers* (should be implies) **3.** ✓ **4.** F
5. *infers* (should be implies) **6.** ✓ **7.** F **8.** ✓
9. ✓ **10.** *imply* (should be infer)

Self-Assessment Log

- Read the directions aloud and have students check vocabulary they learned in the chapter and are prepared to use.
- Have students check the strategies practiced in the chapter (or the degree to which they learned them). They have actually used all these strategies in Chapter 3.
- Put students in small groups. Ask students to find the information or an activity related to each strategy in the group.
- Tell students to find definitions in the chapter for any words they did not check.

Best Practice

Activating Prior Knowledge

Activities such as these help students make text-to-text connections. They have previewed the vocabulary, read it in the passage, and practiced it in the activities. Making up sentences will help the students to use the words in a slightly different context and expand their knowledge. It will also allow the teacher to see if the students have actually learned the words from the chapter.

Expansion Activity

- The aim of this activity is for students to practice writing words in sentences from the **Academic Word List**.
- Tell the students to look at the vocabulary list on page 69 and make up 10 sentences, using as many words as possible.
- Have them take out a piece of paper and begin writing. Give them 10 minutes to complete the activity.
- When they have finished, collect the papers and check them. Tell them you will give a prize to the student who used the most words correctly.
- For variety, have each student write one sentence on the board containing as many words as possible from the list.

CHAPTER 4

Jobs and Professions

In this CHAPTER

Students will read about how work life is changing because of globalization and technology; workers change careers several times in their lives. Some will work at home instead of at a job site, and some are even addicted to work. Then students will read about how people decide what they want to do with their life and how they acquire the necessary skills. If they are not sure, they can consult a career counselor or join a support group. They can also look for jobs on the Internet, either responding to a company's postings or putting their own curricula vitae online. Finally, students will read Peter Drucker's predictions about the rise of two classes in a post-capitalist society, in which some workers will use knowledge as the basis for production and innovation while others will provide services for them, possibly creating a social divide between these two classes.

"Every job is a self-portrait of the person who does it."

Unknown

Chapter Opener

- Direct students' attention to the photo. Then have students work in small groups to answer the questions in the Connecting to the Topic box. Go over the answers as a class.
- Read the quotation and ask students what it means.
- Put two phrases on the board: *Lifetime Job* and *Job Change.*
- Put students in pairs to discuss positive and negative aspects of these situations.
- Call on students to share their ideas with the class.

Chapter Overview

Reading Selections
Changing Career Trends

Looking for Work in the 21st Century

Reading Skills and Strategies
Previewing the topic and vocabulary

Getting meaning from context

Previewing a reading

Identifying the main idea

Identifying important details

Skimming for the topic and the main ideas

Critical-Thinking Skills
Identifying cause and effect

Organizing cause and effect using a graphic organizer

Summarizing a paragraph

Understanding proverbs and quotations

Vocabulary Building
Using the prefix *over-*

Focusing on the Academic Word List

Understanding adjective and noun phrases

Understanding and creating compound words

Language Skills
Understanding pronoun reference

Discussing proverbs and quotations

Identifying challenges and changes within today's work world

Writing a paragraph

Focus on Testing TOEFL® iBT
Increasing reading speed: left-to-right eye movement

Vocabulary

Nouns
- areas*
- benefits*
- career counselors
- cell phones
- computer*
- construction
- drawback
- dream job
- economy*
- employment agency
- globalization*
- identity*
- job hopping
- job security
- labor*
- livelihood
- manufacturing jobs
- outsourcing
- pleasure
- posts
- self-confidence
- stress*
- telecommuting
- workaholism
- workforce

Verbs
- create*
- distract
- keep up with
- overwork
- upgrade
- vary*

Adjectives
- enormous*
- flexible*
- leisure
- passionate
- rigid*
- secure*
- temporary*
- worldwide
- traditionally*

Expression
- on the move

*These words are from the Academic Word List. For more information on this list, see www.victoria.ac.nz/lals/resources/academicwordlist/.

Changing Career Trends

Before You Read

1 Previewing the Topic

- Put students in small groups and have them look at the photos.
- Have students read the questions on page 72 and discuss the answers.
- Call on students to share their answers with the class.
- Write some of the changes on the board and discuss them with the class.

2 Previewing Vocabulary

- Read the directions to the students.
- Have them put a check (✓) next to the words they know.
- Tell them to put the stress on words of more than one syllable as they listen to the audio program.
- Write these words on the board as examples: *globaliza'tion, out'sourcing, keep up' with.*
- Remind them **not** to use a dictionary during this part of the lesson.
- Start the audio.

ANSWER KEY

Nouns

career counselors
cell phones
construction
drawback
globalization
identity
job hopping
job security
livelihood
manufacturing jobs
outsourcing
pleasure
posts
self-confidence
stress
telecommuting
workaholism
workforce

Verbs

distract
keep up with
overwork
upgrade
varies (vary)

Adjectives

flexible
leisure
passionate
rigid
secure
temporary
worldwide

Expression

on the move

3 Getting Meaning from Context

- Read the directions.
- Ask a student to read the first sentence.
- Call on different students to give possible answers.
- If necessary, repeat the process.
- Tell students to continue on their own.

ANSWER KEY

Answers may vary.

1. livelihood = work, job, profession
2. posts = positions, jobs
3. secure = permanent, safe
4. self-confidence = belief in their own ability, self-assurance
5. upgrade = improve, advance
6. keep up with = continue in, maintain skills in
7. telecommuting = work at home, work via the computer, phone
8. distract = take attention away
9. drawback = disadvantage, unfavorable aspect
10. leisure = free time, time away from work
11. globalization = work done all over the world, companies in different countries
12. flexible = changeable, adjusting well to change; rigid = not flexible
13. workaholism = addiction to working, unable to stop working

4 Comparing Answers

- Ask students to take turns reading the sentences and giving answers, which may vary.
- Write any difficult ones on the board if necessary and discuss them.
- Tell students to go back to the vocabulary chart in **Activity 2** and put a check (✓) beside the new words they have just learned.

Strategy

Previewing a Reading

- Write the bullet points from the **Strategy Box** on the board:

  headings—“titles” of paragraphs
  pictures—photos or images
  charts, figures, diagrams

- Read the contents of the **Strategy Box**.
- Tell students to look at the reading “Changing Career Trends” on pages 75–77.
- Point out the headings, the pictures, and the chart.
- Tell them that these will give them an idea of what the reading is about.

5 Previewing a Reading

- Read the directions.
- Ask students the questions.
- Call on different students to give the answers.
- Elicit a few questions from students and write them on the board.

Read

6 Reading an Article

- Write on the board: *What are some ways in which work is changing?*
- Have the students read the passage silently within a time limit (10–15 minutes), or have them follow along as you play the audio.
- Tell them to underline any words or phrases that are new or that they don’t understand.
- Remind them **not** to use a dictionary during this part of the lesson.
- Start the audio.

After You Read

7 Finding the Main Idea

- Read the directions.
- Have different students read each item aloud.
- Ask how many think the main idea is **A**, **B**, **C**, **D**, or **E**.
- Tell those who guessed **C** that they are correct.
- Go over each item and explain that **A**, **B**, **D**, and **E** are about specific topics in the reading, but **C** is the main idea of the reading as a whole.

8 Comprehension Check: Finding Important Details

- Read the directions.
- Have students work in pairs to find the statements that are true according to the reading.
- Check the answers.

ANSWER KEY

1. ✓ **2.** ✓ **4.** ✓ **5.** ✓ **6.** ✓ **8.** ✓

9 Checking Vocabulary

- Read the directions.
- Have the students work individually or in pairs to find the words or expressions.
- Check the answers.

ANSWER KEY

1. career counselors 2. job security
3. outsourcing 4. job hopping 5. drawback

Strategy

Critical Thinking: Recognizing Cause and Effect

- Write on the board:
  causes → effects
  reasons → results
- Read the information in the **Strategy Box**, pointing to the words on the board.

10 Critical Thinking: Recognizing Cause and Effect

Best Practice

Organizing Information

Activities such as this will teach students to organize information from a reading using a graphic organizer. This activity helps students to recognize cause and effect so that they can better understand the reading. In this case, they look up the information and determine the relationships among the facts presented.

- Read the directions.
- Have the students work individually or in pairs to find the causes and effects.
- Check the answers.

ANSWER KEY

Cause	Effect
a decrease in manufacturing jobs	a lack of job security
employers' need to hold down costs	
employers' need to hold down costs	more temporary jobs
	outsourcing
well-educated workforce (in India)	outsourcing to India
salaries are lower	
educated people fluent in English	

FOCUS

Using the Prefix *Over-*

- Write these sentences on the board:
  Some people overwork and don't enjoy their job.
  Other people overeat and gain weight.
  When workers are overtired, they can't perform well.
- Ask students to guess the meaning of the underlined words.
- Read the explanation in the box to the students.
- Ask them what part of speech *overwork* and *overeat* is and write *verb* above them.
- Ask them what part of speech *overtired* is and write *adjective* above it.
- Read the explanation in the box, and tell students that the prefix *over-* can be used with verbs or adjectives.

11 Using the Prefix *Over-*

- Read the directions.
- Check answers after students compare them.
- Point out the difference in spelling and meaning of *overdo* and *overdue*.

ANSWER KEY

1. overdo 2. overcrowded 3. overestimate
4. overdue 5. overpopulation

REPRODUCIBLE Expansion Activity

- The aim of this activity is to help students do collaborative research on the topic of cell phone use. They will share this information with a partner and then with the rest of the class.
- Read the Culture Note in the box and ask students the questions at the end.
- Photocopy and distribute **Black Line Master 10** "Cell Phone Use" on page BLM10 of this Teacher's Manual.
- Tell students to keep a log for one week, showing it to their partner every day.
- When they have finished, have each student make a pie chart from the log, using a simple computer application that generates a display from data input. Tell them to ask for help if they have difficulty.
- Ask a volunteer to gather all the logs and make a pie chart for cell phone use of women and of men in the class, and one of all the logs combined.
- Compare the pie charts to see if there are differences.

Best Practice

Interacting with Others
Activities such as this Expansion Activity will encourage students to work together to gather data. Having to compare logs with a partner will remind them to keep track of phone use. Having to make a pie chart together will help them learn a new computer skill. This will show them that engaging in peer interaction and collaboration will help them academically.

12 Discussing the Reading

- Divide the students into groups, either from the same country or different countries.
- Tell them to choose one person to take notes and another person to share the findings with the class.
- Give them a time limit (10–15 minutes).
- When the time is up, tell them to share the findings with the class.

Looking for Work in the 21st Century

Before You Read

1 Thinking Ahead

- Read the directions.
- Put students in pairs.
- Tell them to answer the questions.
- Have them share their answers with the class.

2 Skimming for the Topic and the Main Idea

- Read the directions.
- Have the students read the passage silently within a time limit (10–15 minutes), or have them follow along as you play the audio.
- After each paragraph, stop the audio and have the students write the topic and main idea of the paragraph.
- Or have them underline the topic and main idea as they're listening, and when the passage is finished, have them discuss their answers with a small group before they write them.
- Remind students **not** to use a dictionary during this part of the lesson.
- Start the audio.

ANSWER KEY

Answers may vary.

A. Topic: Finding a job
Main Idea: In the past, finding a job was a simple process.

B. Topic: Job hunting now is more complex
Main Idea: Now you have to go through more complicated steps to find a new job.

C. Topic: Career counselors
Main Idea: People go to career counselors, who tell them to find a job they love.

D. Topic: Job hunting on the Internet
Main Idea: Many employers advertise jobs online, and many people apply for them.

E. Topic: Job hunting on job boards
Main Idea: People post their résumés on the Internet, and companies can do some of the interviewing online as well.

After You Read

3 Checking Your Answers

- Read the directions.
- Put students in pairs to compare their answers.
- Go around the room and answer questions.

4 Understanding Pronoun Reference

- Read the directions
- Tell the students to work in pairs to find the referents.
- Check the answers with the class.

ANSWER KEY

1. people **2.** professions **3.** their dream job
4. job boards **5.** finding a job on the Internet
6. job interview and skills test

5 Discussing the Reading

- Read the directions.
- Put students into small groups.

- Have them answer the questions together.
- Ask them to share any interesting things they learned with the class.

Content Notes

- *Globalization* has many different meanings. The term is usually used to mean the current socio-economic situation in which capitalism, or the free-market economy, has spread to other countries. Goods and services are provided by people from other countries, so more profits are made.
- Most of the clothes we wear and the items we buy come from other countries. They may be designed in our country, but they are manufactured in another, where the cost of labor is lower. They are shipped and sold all over the world, and many consumers are glad that the cost of these items is lower. However, they are also upset because many factories have closed and jobs have been outsourced, leaving some people unemployed.
- The meaning of *globalization* in the **Cultural Note** on page 84 is slightly different from the above meaning. The five criteria given indicate that it means how well-connected a country is to the rest of the world via cell phones and computers, how involved the citizens are in the politics of the country, how freely other nationalities can move in and out of the country, and now how vibrant the country's economy is.
- Considering this meaning, ask the students to guess which five countries are the most *globalized*. You can put the countries they suggest on the board, and then take a vote. Or students can go to the board and "vote for" five countries by putting a check (✓) after them. When you tally the scores, you can announce the countries:
- ANSWER KEY: 1) Singapore, 2) Ireland, 3) Switzerland, 4) the United States, and 5) the Netherlands.

Best Practice

Making Use of Academic Content

Activities such as this Expansion Activity prepare the students for academic research. By conducting surveys and assembling the data gathered in displays, they will become more familiar with the process and better prepared for academic work.

REPRODUCIBLE

Expansion Activity

- The aim of this activity is for students to do collaborative research on a topic in the chapter. They will share this information with their group and then with the class.
- Photocopy and distribute **Black Line Master 11** "Survey of Globalized Countries" on page BLM11 of this Teacher's Manual.
- Let each group choose a different nationality or age group to survey. Examples of age groups are 20–29, 30–39, 40–49, 50–59, and so on. Have the class agree on either nationality or age group; gender within this category can then be considered.
- Tell students to interview at least 10 people in the category (5 men and 5 women) and record their answers.
- When they are have finished, have students go to the computer lab and make a bar graph with the statistics they have collected. They can use a simple program that automatically builds the graph from the data entered.
- Have them assemble their data displays on a poster board or bulletin board and share their information with the class.

Responding in Writing

6 Summarizing

- Read the directions.
- Assign students to a topic or let them choose one.
- Tell students to sit in small groups and compose a summary together, with each student writing on a separate paper.
- Have one student from each group write the paragraph on the board. Correct any errors.
- If there is time, have the students copy the other two paragraphs from the board after they are corrected.

7 Writing Your Own Ideas

- Assign the paragraph in this section for homework, allowing each student to choose a topic.
- Have each student write the main idea of their paragraph on the line in their books.
- When the students bring their homework in, before you collect it, tell students to exchange papers and read their partner's paragraph.
- Ask them to write the main idea of the summary they have just read under the paragraph.
- When students get their papers back, have them compare their main idea in their books with the one their partners wrote on the papers.
- Collect the papers and correct.

Talk It Over

8 Discussing Proverbs and Quotations

- Read the directions.
- Read the proverbs and quotations to the students and have them repeat them after you.
- Divide students into small groups to discuss the answers to the questions.
- Have them share their ideas with the class.

ANSWER KEY

"*Ninety percent of inspiration is perspiration.*" = [Similar to Thomas Edison's quotation: "*Genius is one percent inspiration and ninety percent perspiration.*"] = A genius (very intelligent person) spends much more time working on her ideas than thinking about them.

"*Work expands to fill up the time available.*" = If we have a month to do a project, it will take a month; if we have only a week, it will take only a week.

"*Laziness travels so slowly that poverty soon overtakes him.*" = If a person is lazy, he will become poor because he doesn't earn enough money to live.

"*It is neither wealth nor splendor, but tranquility and occupation, which give happiness.*" = Being peaceful and occupied (working) makes people happier than being rich or having a fancy lifestyle.

1 Focusing on Words from the Academic Word List

- Read the directions.
- Have students do the activity quickly without using a dictionary.
- For variety, play the audio (first half of paragraph B in "Changing Career Trends") and do the activity as a dictation.
- Have students check the answers on page 75 in the Student Book.

ANSWER KEY

1. varies **2.** economy **3.** traditionally
4. secure **5.** job **6.** job security **7.** jobs
8. enormous **9.** creating **10.** temporary
11. benefits **12.** areas **13.** labor
14. computer

FOCUS

Understanding Adjective and Noun Phrases

- On the board, write *Adjective Phrases* and *Noun Phrases*.
- Under *Adjective Phrases*, write *part-time*, *especially interesting*, and *fastest-growing*.
- Under *Noun Phrases*, write *city life*, *social sciences*, *self-confidence*, and *word-of-mouth*.
- Read the explanation to the class or call on students to read it.
- Call students' attention to the board, and elicit the parts of speech for each word in the phrase, writing the abbreviations, i.e., such as *adj.*, *noun*, and *adv*.
- Tell students that recognizing adjective and noun phrases will help them figure out the meaning of new words.

2 Understanding Adjective and Noun Phrases

- Read the directions.
- Have students do the activity.
- Check the answers.

ANSWER KEY

1. classified/dream
2. unemployment/part/self
3. city/shopping/mass/traffic
4. career/computer
5. job/personnel

3 Creating Adjective and Noun Phrases

- Read the directions.
- Have students do the activity.
- Check the answers.

ANSWER KEY

1. d **2.** a **3.** h **4.** e **5.** b **6.** g
7. c **8.** f

FOCUS

Understanding Compound Words

- Have a student read the explanation and example sentence.
- Have students tell you the two words in each compound word.

  sales + clerk
  super + market

4 Understanding Compound Words

- Read the directions.
- Have students do the activity.
- Check the answers.

ANSWER KEY

1. h over/seas
2. e draw/back
3. j over/crowding
4. a grid/lock
5. i world/wide
6. b over/work
7. c work/force
8. f up/grade
9. d on/line
10. g back/ground

5 Creating Compound Words and Phrases

- Read the directions.
- Have students do the activity in small groups.
- Check the answers.
- Give a prize to the winners.

ANSWER KEY

Answers may vary.

city life	*job interview*	*public college*
city planning	*job market*	*science lab*
college exam	*life science*	*security department*
college tuition	*life work*	*self-confidence*
computer lab	*network security*	*self-service*
high school	*office job*	

6 Searching the Internet

- Ask students if they have ever tried to find a job on the Internet.
- Invite them to share their experiences with the class.
- Direct their attention to this section and read the directions.
- See Expansion Activity.

Best Practice

Cultivating Critical Thinking

Activities such as searching online job boards encourage students to look at Internet use more critically. By evaluating a website, looking at jobs, and actually applying for a position, students can become more familiar with the process and better able to choose an appropriate website in the future.

Reproducible — Expansion Activity

- The aim of this activity is for students to do collaborative research on this topic from the second reading. They will share this information with their group and then each group will share it with the class.
- Photocopy and distribute **Black Line Master 12** "Online Job Boards" on page BLM12 of this Teacher's Manual.
- Print out the following URLs on pieces of paper and let students (in pairs) choose one at random: www.careerbuilder.com; jobsjobsjobs.com; www.jobster.com; www.jobweb.com; www.monster.com.
- Tell students to go to the Computer Lab with their partners or use their own computers after class.
- Have them look up the website and follow the directions.
- When they have finished, have them share their findings with the class.

FOCUS TOEFL® iBT

Faster Reading Speed—Left-to-Right Eye Movement

- Read the directions and go over the **Example** activity.
- Tell students that these exercises activities are especially useful for those whose language is not read left to right, like Arabic (read right to left) and some Asian languages (read top to bottom).

1 Practice

- Read the directions.
- Time students for each section separately.
- At the end, ask them if their time increased, decreased, or stayed the same.

ANSWER KEY

Section 1

banking	banks	banking	bank	banking	banking
challenge	challenges	challenging	challenge	challenge	challenged
savings	savings	save	savings	saving	saver
benefit	benefits	beneficial	benefited	benefit	benefit
employer	employ	employment	employee	employer	employed

Time: ___________

Section 2

experience	experience	experienced	expertise	experience	expert
opening	opening	opening	opened	open	opened
excellent	excel	excelled	excellent	excellent	excellent
identity	indent	identity	identify	identity	indent
account	account	accounting	account	accounts	account

Time: ___________

Section 3

part-time	part-time	partly	party	part-time
position	possible	position	positive	position
public	public	publicity	public	publicize
appointment	appoint	appointed	appoints	appointment
personnel	person	personal	personnel	personable

Time: ___________

Section 4

salary	salary	celery	salaries	salaried	sales
apply	applied	apply	apply	apply	application
pleasure	pleasure	pleasant	pleasurable	pleased	pleasant
skills	skilled	skill	skills	skills	skillful
ability	ability	able	capable	ability	capability

Time: ___________

Self-Assessment Log

- Read the directions aloud and have students check vocabulary they learned in the chapter and are prepared to use.
- Have students check the strategies practiced in the chapter (or the degree to which they learned them). They have actually used all these strategies in Chapter 4.
- Put students in small groups. Ask students to find the information or an activity related to each strategy in the group.
- Tell students to find definitions in the chapter for any words they did not check.

Best Practice

Activating Prior Knowledge

Activities such as this, help students make text-to-text connections. They have previewed the vocabulary, read it in the passage, and practiced it in the activities. Making up paragraphs will help the students use the words in a slightly different context and expand their knowledge. It will also allow the teacher to see if the students have actually learned the words from the chapter. As students check each other's work, they will be reactivating their knowledge as they review an activity similar to the one they have just done.

Expansion Activity

- The aim of this activity is for students to practice writing words in sentences from the **Academic Word List**.
- Have the students look at the vocabulary list on page 91 and tell them each to say a word from the list in order, going through all the words to the end. Tell them to put a check (✓) beside the words they say.
- Have them take out a piece of paper and write a short paragraph containing all the words they checked, underlining the target vocabulary. Give them 10 minutes to complete the activity.
- When they have finished, collect the papers and give them to other students to read. Have the other students check them and write their names at the bottom.
- For variety, have each student write a sentence on the board from the paper that they checked. Collect the papers and check them.

CHAPTER 5

Lifestyles Around the World

In this CHAPTER

Students will read two articles about happiness. The first presents ways that happiness can be measured. The second discusses the relationship of home to happiness. There are opportunities for high-interest discussions around these topics. Students will work on identifying main ideas and creating summaries. They will build vocabulary and work with prefixes and suffixes.

"Learn to be happy with what you have while you pursue all that you want."

Jim Rohn
American entrepreneur, author, and motivational speaker

Chapter Opener

- Direct students' attention to the photo on pages 92–93 of the Student Book and ask: *What does this photo show?* (happy young people) *How do you know?* (smiling, dancing, jumping for joy) Elicit other adjectives to describe their emotions.
- Read the quotation and ask students what it means. Be sure they understand the vocabulary: *entrepreneur, author,* and *motivational speaker.*
- Have students work with a partner or small group to discuss what situations or things make them happy. Ask students to share with the class.

Chapter Overview

Reading Selections
The Science of Happiness

Happiness and the Home

Reading Skills and Strategies
Previewing the topic and vocabulary

Previewing the reading

Identifying the main idea

Identifying acronyms

Getting meaning from context

Marking text when you read

Critical-Thinking Skills
Interpreting source material from the Internet

Studying for exams: organizing information

Understanding italics

Summarizing a paragraph

Vocabulary Building
Focusing on the Academic Word List

Analyzing prefixes and suffixes

Understanding dictionary entries: words with single and multiple meanings

Language Skills
Discussing happiness and how it is measured

Writing a paragraph

Focus on Testing TOEFL® iBT
Focusing on vocabulary questions

Vocabulary

Nouns
- areas*
- balance
- concept*
- components*
- constitution*
- environment*
- essence
- findings
- gap
- income*
- life expectancy
- polls
- researchers*
- solidarity
- sum total
- trend*
- well-being

Verbs
- catch on
- measure

Adjectives
- complex*
- economic*
- mental*
- psychological*
- reasonable

Adverbs
- actually
- enthusiastically

*These words are from the Academic Word List. For more information on this list, see www.victoria.ac.nz/lals/resources/academicwordlist/.

The Science of Happiness

Before You Read

1 Previewing the Topic

- Put students in small groups and have them look at the map. Tell them to ask and answer the questions.
- Call on students to share their answers with the class.
- Write a few comments they may have about the map on the board.

2 Previewing Vocabulary

- Read the directions to students.
- Have them read the words and phrases to themselves. Then play the audio so that they can hear the pronunciation.
- Tell students to put a check mark (✓) next to the words they know.
- Tell students **not** to use a dictionary during this part of the lesson.

3 Previewing the Reading

- Read the questions and call on students to answer them.
- Comment on the answers, if necessary.

ANSWER KEY

1. The Science of Happiness
2. Human Development Index, What's Missing from the HDI, Happiness and Bhutan, The Spread of This Concept, A New Measure, What Happiness is—and Isn't, Conclusion
3. Answers will vary.

Read

4 Reading an Article

- Write on the board: *How is the happiness of a nation measured?* and ask students to think about this question as they read.
- Have students read the passage silently within a time limit (10–15 minutes), or have them follow along as you play the audio.
- Tell them to underline any words or phrases that are new or that they don't understand. Remind them **not** to use a dictionary during this part of the lesson.
- Tell student to do **Activity 5 Finding the Main Idea** when they finish the reading.

After You Read

5 Finding the Main Idea

- Read the directions.
- Call on different students to read the answer choices.
- Ask which one is correct.

ANSWER KEY

C: Measuring the happiness of a nation or person is complex.

6 Identifying the Main Idea in Paragraphs

- Read the directions. Tell students to look back at the reading and underline one or two sentences in each paragraph that contain the main idea.
- If students finish quickly, have them compare their answers with a partner.
- Check the answers as a class.

ANSWER KEY

A: Increasingly, there is understanding that GDP is not enough of a measure of a nation's well-being.

B: Since 1993, the United Nations has used the HDI, or Human Development Index, to measure the well-being of a nation.

C: The HDI does not reflect most of these areas.

D: The idea is that happiness is far more complex than economic growth.

E: This concept of measuring GNH is catching on worldwide.

F: As this concept of GNH becomes more popular, there is an effort to find a new, global measure for well-being.

G: We have learned a lot in recent years about what makes a happy person or a happy nation.

H: It is possible to measure the happiness of a nation, but it is challenging.

Strategy

Understanding Acronyms

- Read the information in the Strategy box with students.
- Provide some other examples for your students and ask them to share acronyms that they may know.

7 Checking Acronyms

- Have students quickly scan the reading passage for the acronyms and give their meanings.

ANSWER KEY

GDP: Gross Domestic Product, HDI: Human Development Index, GNH: Gross National Happiness, GNW: Gross National Wellness

8 Checking Your Understanding

- Read the directions and repeat the question: *How is the happiness of a nation measured?*
- Have students discuss the answer with their partner.
- Have pairs share their answers with another pair.

ANSWER KEY

Answers will vary.

Best Practice

Interacting with Others

Activities such as the Expansion Activity below will encourage students to use language for real-life communication and add variety to the class. Interviewing people, asking questions, and sharing information with each other and the class will foster fruitful interaction and meaningful language practice.

REPRODUCIBLE

Expansion Activity

- Photo copy and distribute **Black Line Master 13** "Happiness Poll" from page BLM13 in this Teacher's Manual.
- Tell students to interview five students and ask them to rate the qualities of happiness in their country. They should use the adjectives *good, average, poor.*
- Tell students to take notes during the interview.
- Give them a few days to complete the assignment if needed.
- When they finish, have them share their findings with the class.
- Compare the information to see if there are any similarities or differences in the poll results.
- Collect students' work and comment.

9 Getting Meaning from Context: Vocabulary Check

- Read the directions.
- Ask students to repeat the words after you.
- Review the Tip box "Getting Meaning from Context" in the margin on Student Book page 99.
- Put students in pairs and give them a time limit (10 minutes) to find the words.
- Check the answers together with the class.

ANSWER KEY

1. prosperity or happiness
2. parts
3. how long people expect to live
4. idea
5. general direction of change
6. agreement among people
7. ways to help people in difficult situations
8. suggestion
9. result of research
10. a central quality

10 Finding Details

- Read the directions.
- Tell students to form pairs and find the answers together.
- Have them compare their answers with another pair of students.

ANSWER KEY

Drawbacks of GDP: disasters and social ills can increase GDP, it doesn't identify income gaps, it doesn't measure happiness

Components of HDI: income, education, life expectancy

Countries with the highest levels of satisfaction: Denmark, Finland, Netherlands, Sweden

11 Discussing the Reading

- Read the directions.
- Direct students to work in small groups.
- Have students check the answers with another group.

ANSWER KEY

1. Answers will vary.
2. Pie chart segments: economic, environmental, physical, mental, workplace, social, political
3. Answers will vary.
4. Answers will vary.

Using the Internet

Interpreting Source Material from the Internet

- Read the information with students.
- Discuss various websites and their sources. Remind students that URLs ending in *.gov*, *.mil* (military), or *.edu*, and some ending in *.org* are usually reputable. Reputable sites usually have a "Contact Us" or "About Us" link where you can learn about the website's sponsoring organization. Another way to determine accuracy is to verify the date that the site was last updated.

12 Searching the Internet

- Read the instructions with students.
- If you have Internet access in your classroom, you may wish to do this activity together with your students. If not, direct students to the computer lab or their home computers to complete the tasks.
- Remind them to record the URLs where they found the information.
- Have students compare their findings.

Happiness and the Home

Before You Read

1 Thinking Ahead

- Read the directions.
- Ask students to work with a partner to answer the questions.
- Write some of their responses on the board.

Strategy

Marking Text When You Read

- Bring several highlighters to class, or ask students to bring them.
- Read the information in the Strategy box.
- Ask students how they use highlighters.
- Encourage those who don't use highlighters to bring them to their classes and use them when reading.

Read

2 Reading: Marking Text When You Read

- Read the instructions with students.
- Draw their attention to the Reading Tip box.
- Instruct students to mark their books during this activity.
- Tell students who don't have highlighters to underline, circle, or make notes in the margin.

ANSWER KEY

Answers will vary. Sample answers:

A. Topic: home
Main Idea: A home is both a physical space and all that we associate with it.

B. Topic: home design
Main Idea: Home design and building materials are based on where we live.

C. Topic: home is hearth
Main Idea: Fire in the hearth means cooking and comfort.

D. Topic: home as expression of personal identity
Main Idea: Home can be physical or virtual. It's where people are possibly the happiest.

After You Read

3 Checking Your Answers

- Read the directions.
- Have students work with a partner to compare and refine their Topics and Main Ideas for the reading selection.
- Circulate among the pairs and have students share the best options with the class.

FOCUS

Understanding Italics

- Read the information with students.
- Go over the Example.

ANSWER KEY

happiness = to mean the word; *Ataraxia* = foreign language term; *gaoxing* = foreign language term; *do* = for emphasis; *be* = for emphasis

4 Understanding Italics

- Read the instructions.
- Have students compare their answers with a classmate.

ANSWER KEY

Paragraph A: *home* = to mean the word; *and* = for emphasis; *home* = to mean the word

Paragraph B: *lobembe, gher,* and *tsagaan* are all foreign language terms

Paragraph C: *kotatsu* = foreign language term; *all* = for emphasis; *hearth* = to mean the word

Paragraph D: *chotchkies* = foreign language term

Strategy

Studying for Exams: Organizing Information

- Read the directions.
- Demonstrate each step using this book, a notebook, and a sketch of a graphic organizer on the board. Refer students to the graphic organizers on Student Book pages 30–31, 55, and 79.

5 Studying for Exams: Organizing Information

Best Practice

Organizing Information

Activities such as this will teach students to organize information from a reading passage using a graphic organizer. This allows students to better assimilate and recall information. In this case, students make note of topic, main idea, and important details.

- Read the directions.
- Have students complete the chart.
- Divide students into groups of three to discuss their answers.
- Select some groups to share their answers with the class.

ANSWER KEY

Answers may vary.

	Topic	Main Idea	Important Details
A	home	A home is both a physical space and all that we associate with it.	• family • security • comfort • beauty • food • family history
B	home design	Home design and building materials are based on where we live.	• made of products available: wood, plants, skins, stone • color is meaningful in Greece
C	home is hearth	Fire in the hearth means cooking and comfort.	• in Japan sit around table • Pygmies sit around fire • food • safety • kitchen (hearth) is emotional center
D	home as expression of identity	A home is where people are possibly the happiest.	• can be virtual or physical • choose furnishings • secure, comfortable, relaxed

6 Discussing the Reading

- Go over the instructions and tasks.
- You may wish to have students discuss Items 1, 2, 3, and 4 in small groups. Have each group assign a recorder to report their findings to the class.
- For Item 5, discuss each proverb as a whole class activity.
- Have students share similar proverbs from their language and country.

Responding in Writing

7 Summarizing

- Read the directions.
- Ask two students to read Summary 1 and Summary 2.
- Have them compare the summaries with Paragraph A on page 101 of the Student Book.

ANSWER KEY

Similarities: "Home" is defined in the same way in both Summary 1 and Summary 2.

Both summaries contain the Main Idea: a house is both a physical space and all that we associate with it.

Differences: Summary 1 includes different details than Summary 2. Summary 2 doesn't include important details.

8 Writing Your Own Summary

- Tell students to choose one of the paragraphs listed to summarize.
- Remind them not to look at the original paragraph as they are writing. Tell those who have chosen Paragraphs B and C to look at the graphic organizer on page 105 in their Student Book to help them with their summary.
- Allow students a time limit (10–15 minutes) to complete this activity.
- Have students who worked on the same paragraph compare their summaries when finished.
- Collect summaries and check.

9 Writing a Response

Best Practice

Activating Prior Knowledge

An activity such as writing a summary in class enables students to be more successful when they work at home. This activity uses prior practice as a scaffold, enabling students to be more successful when they write a summary by themselves.

- Assign this activity for homework, allowing each student to choose a topic.
- Tell students to write the main idea on the line in their books.
- Before you collect the homework, tell students to exchange papers and read their partner's paragraph. Ask them to write the main idea under the paragraph.
- When students get their papers back from their partners, have them compare their main idea with the one their partners wrote under their paragraph.
- Collect the papers and correct them.

1 Focusing on Words from the Academic Word List

- Read the directions.
- Say the words and have students repeat them after you.
- Ask them what part of speech the words are, and tell them to write *n.*, *v.*, *adj.*, or *adv.* after the words.

areas = *n.*
complex = *adj.*
concept = *n.*
constitution = *n.*
Economic = *adj.*
environment = *n.*
income = *n.*
mental = *adj.*
psychological = *adj.*
researchers = *n.*

- Remind them to cross off the words from the list as they fill in the blanks.
- Have students check their answers with a classmate.

ANSWER KEY

1. Economic
2. mental
3. researchers
4. income
5. areas
6. complex
7. concept
8. constitution
9. psychological
10. environment

FOCUS

Analyzing Suffixes

- Write the examples from the Focus box on the board.

Nouns	**Verbs**	**Adverb**
-ity	*-ate*	*-ly*
-ship	*-ize*	

- Read the information in the Focus box with students.
- Ask individuals to go to the board and write some words in the columns containing these suffixes. (Answers will vary.)

2 Analyzing Suffixes

- Read the directions.
- Remind students **not** to use a dictionary during this activity.
- Check the answers when students have finished.

ANSWER KEY

1. *n.* friendship
2. *adj.* universal
3. *n.* apartment
4. *n.* security
5. *adv.* exactly
6. *n.* expression
7. *adj.* additional
8. *v.* balance (or *n.*)
9. *adv.* enthusiastically
10. *adj.* expensive
11. *v.* associate (or *n.*)
12. *adj.* traditional
13. *v.* summarize
14. *adv.* frequently
15. *n.* satisfaction
16. *adj.* physical (or *n.*)
17. *n.* environment
18. *n.* ability
19. *n.* organization
20. *adv.* actually
21. *n.* solidarity
22. *n.* essence
23. *adj.* reasonable
24. *adj.* central

FOCUS

Analyzing Prefixes

- Write the example from the Focus box on the board: *We've discovered many unusual and interesting houses in our travels.*
- Read the information in the box and underline *dis* and *un* in the words *discovered* and *unusual.*
- Write the prefixes from the box in columns on the board, without their definitions: *un-, in-, im-, ir-, dis-.*
- Ask students to go to the board and write some words in the columns containing these prefixes, or elicit words from students.

3 Analyzing Prefixes

- Read the directions.
- Check answers with students when finished.

ANSWER KEY

1. un **2.** dis **3.** in **4.** un **5.** in **6.** un
7. un **8.** in **9.** un **10.** un **11.** im **12.** un

FOCUS

More Prefixes

- Write the prefixes from the Focus box on the bottom of Student Book page 109 without the meanings.
- Explain that these prefixes come from Latin and that many Latinate languages (French, Italian, Portuguese, and Spanish) have similar prefixes.
- Draw students' attention to the meanings listed in the Focus box.
- Have students suggest words that they know for each prefix. Write them next to the appropriate prefixes.

Best Practice

Scaffolding Instruction
The activity in the Focus notes above uses students' prior knowledge as a scaffold. It helps them place what they already know about prefixes in their own language into the understanding and use of prefixes in English.

4 Matching Words

- Read the directions.
- Remind students to cross off the definitions as they use them.
- Have students do this activity without using a dictionary.
- Check answers together.

ANSWER KEY

1. e **2.** i **3.** j **4.** c **5.** a **6.** b **7.** h
8. d **9.** f **10.** g

FOCUS

Understanding Dictionary Entries: Single and Multiple Meanings

- Read the information in the Focus box.
- Go over the multiple meanings of *cry* (verb and noun), *home* (hearth, house), *support* (noun and verb), *watch* (noun and verb).

5 Understanding Dictionary Entries: Single Meanings

- Read the directions.
- Have two students read the two dictionary entries aloud or have students read them silently.
- Ask other students to answer the questions in the activity.

ANSWER KEY

1. noun
2. a tall, heavy, plant-eating mammal of tropical Africa and south central Asia, with a long, flexible prehensile trunk, ivory tusks, and large ears.
3. adjective
4. happening, appearing, or being made not long ago; new, modern

6 Understanding Dictionary Entries: Multiple Meanings

- Read the directions.
- Ask several students to read the dictionary entries, or tell students to read them silently.
- Ask other students to answer the questions.

ANSWER KEY

1. noun, answers will vary
2. 5, 6
3. **a.** verb, 6
   b. noun, 5
   c. noun, 3
   d. verb, 3
4. **a.** to maintain financially
   b. evidence for a story, statement or idea
   c. person or thing that gives aid
   d. to give approval to a decision, idea, or cause

7 Dictionary Practice

Best Practice

Making Use of Academic Content
Activities such as this will help expand students' use of the dictionary from a mere translator into a more useful tool that can help them learn about parts of speech, different meanings of words, and examples.

- Read the directions
- Tell students to work as quickly as possible.
- If students finish quickly, have them check their answers with a partner.

ANSWER KEY

1. *noun*, an environment of comfort, security, and happiness
2. *adj.*, relating to a place of origin or residence
3. *vt.*, to cover in the same way as a blanket
4. *noun*, a large piece of textile usually found on a bed
5. *vt.*, to provoke emotions of sadness, joy, or connection
6. *noun*, an action or act in a game or in life

8 Searching the Internet

- Read the directions.
- Have students work independently or in pairs, in the computer lab or resource center, or at home.
- Tell them to be sure to record the URL for the Internet sites. Print out a photo if they can.
- If you have Internet access in your classroom, have students show their websites to the class.
- Have students answer the questions and report to the class.

FOCUS TOEFL® iBT

Vocabulary Questions on the TOEFL® iBT

- Read the information to students.
- Tell students that the following activity will help them prepare for the TOEFL®iBT

1 Practice

- Read the directions.
- Write *Happiness and the Home, pages 101–103* on the board.
- Put the current time and the time in 10 minutes on the board, for example, 10:30–10:40, explaining that this is a timed activity.
- Tell students to begin the Practice when you say "Start," and to work as quickly as possible.
- Tell students to stop working when the time is up.
- You may wish to review the correct answers for the Practice activity.

ANSWER KEY

1. C **2.** D **3.** C **4.** B **5.** A
6. D **7.** C **8.** B

Self-Assessment Log

- Read the directions aloud and have students check vocabulary they learned in the chapter and are prepared to use.
- Have students check the strategies practiced in the chapter, or the degree to which they learned them.
- Put students in small groups. Ask students to find the information or an activity related to each strategy in the list.
- Tell students to find definitions in the chapter and learn any words they did not check.

Best Practice

Interacting with Others

Activities such as the Expansion Activity below will energize students and add excitement to the class. Since most interaction in this chapter has been in pairs or small groups, students will enjoy a change of pace with some competitive interaction.

Expansion Activity

- Write all the words from the Vocabulary list on separate pieces of paper.
- Divide students into 4 groups, and give each group 4 pieces of paper with words from the list. Tell students not to let the other groups know which words they have.
- Tell students to look up their words in a dictionary and write the meanings on the back of each piece of paper.
- Have each group go to the board and write the definition of one of the words.
- Tell the other groups to guess the word without looking at the list.
- The group that guesses the word first gets a point and puts one of their definitions on the board.
- Repeat this process until none of the groups have any more words.
- Tally the score at the end. The team with the highest score wins.
- If it's not possible for students to go to the board, tell them to stand up and say the definition. Have the groups guess the word.

CHAPTER 6

Global Connections

In this CHAPTER

Students will learn about the globalization of our food supply and developments that endanger the diversity of what we eat. The second reading expands the theme of globalization to television and the worldwide phenomenon of reality TV. Students will have the opportunity to research using the Internet and to present their views about the impact of our global connections.

Chapter Opener

- Direct students' attention to the background photo on pages 116–117. Ask if they have seen grocery displays like this. What foods are shown?
- Have a student read the headline and text in the brochure on pages 116–117. Check for comprehension by asking: *What is the brochure advertising?* (TV show contest for the world's best chef) *Do you watch cooking shows on TV? Do you watch competition shows on TV?* Which ones? You may wish to bring in a cookbook or product sponsored by a famous TV chef.
- Discuss the questions in item 3 in the Connecting to the Topic box with the class.
- Read the quotation and ask students what it means. Remind them to look for the root words for vocabulary they don't know.

"We… have a cultural phenomenon: the emergence of a global culture, or cultural globalization."

Peter L. Berger
Austrian-American sociologist

Chapter Overview

Reading Selections
Globalization and Food

Life in a Fishbowl: Globalization and Reality TV

Reading Skills and Strategies
Previewing the topic and vocabulary

Previewing the reading

Identifying main ideas

Skimming for main ideas

Critical-Thinking Skills
Understanding the literal and figurative meanings of words

Organizing information using an outline

Summarizing in writing

Understanding inferences

Vocabulary Building
Understanding idioms and figurative language

Focusing on the Academic Word List

Focusing on expressions and idioms

Using participles as adjectives

Language Skills
Stating and explaining opinions

Writing a paragraph

Focus on Testing TOEFL® iBT
Identifying inferences

Vocabulary

Nouns
- access*
- areas*
- benefit*
- chemicals*
- concept*
- consumer*
- extinction
- fuel
- globalization*
- livestock
- nutrients
- obstacle
- region*
- shift*
- staples

Verbs
- contribute*
- shift*

Adjectives
- endangered
- processed*
- traditional*

Adverb
- approximately*

Expression
- in turn

*These words are from the Academic Word List. For more information on this list, see www.victoria.ac.nz/lals/resources/academicwordlist/.

Globalization and Food

Before You Read

1 Previewing the Topic

- Put students in small groups and have them discuss the questions.
- Call on students to share their answers with the class. Their answers may vary.

2 Previewing Vocabulary

- Read the directions to students.
- Have them read the words and phrases to themselves. Then play the audio so that they can hear the pronunciation.
- Tell students to put a check mark (✓) next to the words they know.
- Tell students **not** to use a dictionary during this part of the lesson.

3 Previewing the Reading

- Read the questions and have students work in pairs to answer them.
- Give students a time limit of 5 minutes to answer the questions.
- Call on students to answer the questions so that you can check their answers. Comment on the answers, if necessary.

ANSWER KEY

1. globalization and food
2. Our Diet Today, Loss of Variety, Causes of Disappearing Varieties, The Story of Two Crops, Localization—The Solution
3. Answers will vary.

Read

4 Reading an Article

- Read the directions.
- Write *"How—and why—is our diet changing?"* on the board. Ask students to think about this question as they are reading.
- Remind students to look at the photos and graphics to help them understand what they are reading.
- Have students read the passage silently within a time limit (10–15 minutes) or have them follow along silently as you play the audio.
- Tell them to underline any words or phrases that are new or that they don't understand. Remind them **not** to use a dictionary during this part of the lesson.
- Tell students to look at the activity following the reading if they finish quickly.

After You Read

5 Finding the Main Idea

- Read the directions.
- Give students five minutes to work through the statements alone.
- Then, have a student read statement 1.
- Have students raise their hands if they feel statement 1 is true. Then have them raise their hands if they believe it is false.
- Continue with the rest of the statements.

ANSWER KEY

1. T **2.** T **3.** F **4.** T **5.** F **6.** T

Strategy

Understanding the Literal and Figurative Meanings of Words

- Write the following on the board:

  literal = letters   *figurative = form or figure*

- Then write on the board: *"The diseased seeds in the farmer's hand planted a seed of worry in his mind."*
- Explain the difference in the literal meaning of "seed" and the figurative meaning of "seed" in this example. Compare the tiny kernel that grows into a plant to the tiny worry that will grow in the farmer's mind.
- Tell students that they will encounter many words that have both literal and figurative meanings.

6 Understanding the Literal and Figurative Meanings of Words

- Read the directions. Tell student to look back in the reading to find the answers. Give them a time limit (10 minutes).
- Check the answers with the class.

ANSWER KEY

1. C **2.** D **3.** B **4.** D **5.** B **6.** E **7.** A

7 Checking Vocabulary

- Read the directions.
- Check the answers with the class.

ANSWER KEY

1. benefit **2.** shift **3.** contributes **4.** fuel
5. in turn **6.** obstacle **7.** consumers
8. nutrients **9.** extinction **10.** priority
11. livestock

8 Checking Your Understanding

- Read the directions.
- Discuss the answers that students give and write some of them on the board.

Strategy

Understanding Outlines

- Read the information about outlines in the Strategy box.
- Write the first section of the outline on the board:

  Globalization and Food

  I. Introduction: The World's Changing Diet

  A. Always changing

  1. Banana from India to Greece, about 350 B.C.

  2. Potato from South America to Europe, 1570

  3. From there to the rest of the world

  B. Globalization changing our diet faster now

- Ask a student to read Paragraph A on page 119. Tell student to listen and look at the outline on the board.
- Point out the phrases on the board as the student reads them.
- Ask these questions and tell students to answer them using phrases on the board: *Is our changing diet new?* (No, it has always been changing.) *What are two examples from the past?* (The banana came from India to Greece about 350 B.C. and the potato came from South America to Europe in 1570.) *What is the difference in the changes today?* (Globalization is changing our diet faster now.)
- Read the rest of the outline aloud as students follow along.

9 Understanding Outlines

Best Practice

Organizing Information
Activities such as this will teach students to organize information using an outline. This allows students to identify main ideas and supporting details from sections of text and put the information into a format that facilitates review at a later date.

- Read the directions.
- Tell students to do the activity using the outline on pages 124–125.

ANSWER KEY

1. globalization and food
2. banana, potato
3. IV.A, Farmers replacing traditional varieties (key reason), IV.B. Big industrial agriculture, and IV.C. Seed industry
4. V.A. Potato—in the past, V.B. Banana today
5. VI.A. The "Buy Local" movement
   VI.B. Organizations collecting seeds of endangered varieties

10 Finding the Main Idea

- Read the directions.
- Call on different student to read the answer choices.
- Elicit the answer (B). Note that answer C has two main ideas.

11 Discussing the Reading

- Read the directions for Activity 11, questions 1, 3, and 4. Tell students that item 2 will be done as an Internet activity later.
- Divide students into pairs or small groups to discuss these three questions.
- Go around the room and listen to the discussions. Facilitate where needed.
- Ask students to share their ideas with the class.
- Draw students' attention to item 2 in this activity. You may want to copy **Blackline Master 14, Analyzing a Country's Endangered Food**, found on page BLM14 in this Teacher's Manual, for students to use a research guide and to expand the activity. Have students go to the computer lab or work independently at home to complete their Internet research.
- Follow up on this activity by having students share their findings with the class.
- Collect their research notes and check.

Best Practice

Cultivating Critical Thinking
Activities such as the one on **Black Line Master 14** allow students to engage in critical thinking as they consider the current state of food in countries around the world. By doing research on the Internet and identifying a country's endangered resources they will be better able to formulate ideas about ways to protect biodiversity.

Life in a Fishbowl: Globalization and Reality TV

Before You Read

1 Thinking Ahead

Best Practice

Scaffolding Instruction

Activities such as this will allow students to better understand a reading by scaffolding instruction. Eliciting information that students already know will enable them to understand new information and integrate it with prior knowledge.

- Read the directions.
- Create this graphic organizer on the board. Fill it in with student responses to the questions in the activity.

Favorite TV programs	Reality TV favorites	YouTube favorites

- Discuss the similarities and differences between the information.

Read

2 Skimming for Main Ideas

- Read the directions.
- Give students a time limit (10–15 minutes) or turn on the audio.
- Check students' answers.

ANSWER KEY

Paragraph A: B
Paragraph B: D
Paragraph C: A
Paragraph D: E
Paragraph E: E

After You Read

FOCUS

Understanding Idioms

- Write the example sentence on the board: *"For the family on a reality TV show, it was life in a fishbowl."* Underline "in a fishbowl."
- Have a student read the first paragraph in the Focus box.
- Read the second paragraph in the Focus box, using the example on the board.

3 Understanding Idioms and Figurative Language

- Read the directions.
- You may want to have students do the activity in pairs.
- Go around the room and help students with the answers if needed.

ANSWER KEY

1. tearjerkers
2. to rough it
3. out-of-the-way
4. kicked out
5. battle each other
6. it goes without saying
7. a good deal
8. chances are
9. spreading like wildfire
10. fought tooth and nail
11. go viral
12. rags-to-riches

Responding in Writing

4 Summarizing

- Read the directions.
- Give students a minute to decide which part of which reading they will summarize.
- Ask students who are going to summarize a paragraph from Part 1 to sit on one side of the room. Ask students who are going to summarize a paragraph from Part 2 to sit on the other side of the room.
- Write these two pieces of advice on the board: *"A summary is shorter than the original."* and *"Don't look at the original paragraph as you write."*
- Put students in pairs. They can first write the summary alone, and then compare their summary with that of their partner.
- When they have compared their summaries, collect the summaries and check them.

5 Writing Your Own Ideas

Best Practice

Interacting with Others
Activities such as this will encourage students to use language for real-life communication and add variety to the class. Writing persuasive paragraphs for a classmate and getting a response to that writing will foster meaningful interaction and interesting language practice.

- Read the directions.
- Have students choose one of the topics listed and write the two paragraphs for homework.
- The next day, collect students' work.
- Distribute each student's writing to a different student in the class. Make sure no one gets his or her own paragraphs.
- Tell students to read them and write the main idea of each paragraph at the bottom or on the back of the paper.
- Then have students write a response to their classmates writing. They should write their reaction to the writer's opinion.
- When students finish, they give the paper back to the person who wrote it.
- After reading what their classmate has written, students should turn their paper in to you for your review.

6 Discussing the Reading

- Read the directions.
- Divide students into small groups to discuss the answers.
- Have them share their answers with the class.

7 Searching the Internet

- Read the directions.
- Direct students to use the computer lab or work on their own computer.
- Remind them to make note of the URLs where they find their information. They should also include the date they accessed the site.
- If students choose to research a Reality TV Show, photocopy **Blackline Master 15 Reality TV Shows,** on page BLM15 in this Teacher's Manual. Review the instructions on the worksheet.
- Students who are researching the psychology of people who watch or are contestants on reality programs should keep a log of their web search and write a summary of their findings. If possible, they can print out a copy of their article and attach it to their summary.
- Instruct students to find someone who worked on the same task and compare their findings.
- After students have shared their research, collect their work and check.

1 Focusing on Words from the Academic Word List

- Read the directions.
- Say the words and have students repeat them after you.
- Ask them what part of speech they are and tell them to write *n, v, adj,* or *adv* after the words.

  access (n), areas (n), chemicals (n), concept (n), consumers (n), globalization (n), processed (adj), region (n), shift (n), traditional (adj)

- Tell them to cross off the words from the list as they use them. One word will be used twice.

ANSWER KEY

1. concept **2.** region **3.** globalization
4. access **5.** areas **6.** consumers **7.** shift
8. traditional **9.** processed **10.** chemicals
11. traditional

2 Expressions and Idioms

- Read the directions.
- Say the expressions and have students repeat them after you.
- Remind students **not** to use a dictionary during this activity and to cross out the idioms as they use them. Alert students that they will not use all the expressions.
- Check the answers as a class.

ANSWER KEY

1. roughing it
2. spread like wildfire / went viral
3. all corners of the world
4. Chances are
5. It goes without saying
6. rags-to-riches
7. out-of-the-way
8. fight tooth and nail

FOCUS

Using Participles as Adjectives

- Write the following on the board.

Present Participle	**Past Participle**
-ing = cause of emotion	*-ed* = effect or result
That book is *interesting.*	I'm *interested* in that book.
We watched a *boring* movie.	We were so *bored* that we fell asleep.
The race was *tiring.*	The runners were *tired* after it.

- Read the information in the Focus box and review the chart on the board.
- Call on two students to read the **Examples**.

3 Using Participles as Adjectives

- Read the directions.
- Read the words and have students give you the present and past participle. For example, when you say *challenge,* students say *challenging* and *challenged.* (disgusting/disgusted; embarrassing/embarrassed; encouraging/encouraged; entertaining/entertained; exciting/excited; horrifying/horrified; interesting/interested)
- Have students work on the activity in pairs. Remind them to check off the words as they use them.

ANSWER KEY

1. entertained, entertaining, disgusting
2. horrifying, encouraging
3. interested, challenging
4. exciting, excited, embarrassed

FOCUS TOEFL® iBT

Understanding Inferences

- Read the paragraph to students.
- Tell students that they will do three activities that will help them prepare for the TOEFL®iBT.

1 Practice

- Read the directions, emphasizing that each item has more than one answer.
- Write *"Globalization and Food, pages 119–121"* on the board.
- Put the current time on the board and the time in 10 minutes, for example 10:30–10:40.
- Tell students to begin the activity, working as quickly as possible.

ANSWER KEY

1. B, E **2.** A, B **3.** A, B, D, E **4.** B, C, D, E

2 Distinguishing Stated from Inferred Information

- Read the directions.
- Have students mark "S" or "I" next to the statements in Activity 1.
- When finished, direct them to compare their answers with a partner.
- Review the answers with the class.

ANSWER KEY

1. B = stated, E = stated

2. A = stated, B = stated

3. A = stated, B = inferred, D = stated, E = stated

4. B = stated, C = inferred, D = inferred, E = inferred

3 Critical Thinking: Identifying Inferences

Best Practice

Making Use of Academic Content
Activities such as this will help expand students' understanding of inference in academic texts. With practice, they will learn to recognize what can be inferred from factual information.

- Read the instructions.
- Read the first item together: *Global culture these days does not have much variety.*
- Ask students if this statement is stated in the reading passage. (no) Ask if it can be inferred from the passage? (no)
- Remind students that they should not consider whether the statement is true or false, but rather if it is inferred in the reading.
- When students have completed the activity, review their responses as a whole class activity.

ANSWER KEY

Answers may vary.

Paragraph A:

2. ✓ countries influence each other's food, music, education, technology, fashion, and entertainment

3. ✓ a form of entertainment that has spread to all corners of the world

Paragraph B:

2. ✓ Most typical reality TV shows are competitions.

4. ✓ *Extremely dangerous, disgusting, painful* are adjectives the writer uses to describe the show.

Paragraph C:

4. ✓ Examples: *Canadian Idol, Malaysian Idol, Vietnam Idol, Nouvelle Star in* France, *Super Idol* in the Arab world

Paragraph D:

1. ✓ could only watch once per week, at home on TV

2. ✓ now available round-the-clock and on Internet, on demand

4. ✓ can subscribe to watch anytime and on many devices, even a cell phone

Paragraph E:

3. ✓ "It's quite possible" viewers enjoy watching the failure of contestant they dislike; punishment, revenge for those with character flaws

4. ✓ Final sentence: "The desire to see the "good guy" win and the "bad guy" lose seems to reflect universal human values."

Self-Assessment Log

- Read the directions aloud and have students check vocabulary they learned in the chapter and are prepared to use.
- Have students check the strategies practiced in the chapter (or the degree to which they learned them). They have actually used all of these strategies in Chapter 6.
- Put students in small groups. Ask students to find the information or an activity related to each strategy in the chapter.
- Tell students to find definitions in the chapter for any words they did not check.

REPRODUCIBLE

Expansion Activity

- Write the expressions from the left column of Part 2, Activity 3 Understanding Idioms and Figurative Language on page 131.
- Write the words from the right column on separate pieces of paper and distribute them to students or pairs of students, depending on the number in the class. Add other words from the list if necessary.
- Divide students into two teams, making sure they keep their books closed.
- Tell them to look at the expressions on the board and allow one student or pair to go to the board to write their idiom next to the definition on the board.
- If it's not possible for students to go to the board, read the sentences aloud one by one and have students stand up and say their idiom if it fits the sentence.
- If it is correct, give the student/team one point, and have a member/pair of the other team go to the board next.
- Repeat the process until neither team has any more words.
- Tally the score at the end. The team with the highest score wins.
- Photocopy and distribute **Black Line Master 16 Matching Idioms** on page BLM16 in this Teacher's Manual.
- Instruct students to copy down the answers on the Black Line Master worksheet and study for the chapter test.

CHAPTER 7

Language and Communication

In this CHAPTER

Students will read about different aspects of language and communication, such as how animals communicate, how human communication differs according to gender, and finally, how English i[s] changing as it spreads around the world. In the first reading, they wil[l] learn about the communication of insects through smell and sight, th[e] vocalizations of prairie dogs and dolphins, the ability of chimpanzees to communicate through body language and manipulation of symbols like humans. They will explore the differences between male and female styles of communication, as studied by the noted linguist, Deborah Tannen, and discuss these differences with their classmate[s]. At the end of the chapter, they will learn of the dismay of linguists at the morphing of the Queen's English into different hybrids around the world. These topics will encourage students to think about modes of communication among animals and humans as well as the language they are in the process of acquiring.

Chapter Opener

- Direct students' attention to the photo. Then have students work in small groups to answer the questions in the Connecting to the Topic box. Go over the answers as a class.
- Read the quotation by Whorf and ask students what it means.
- Put this sentence on the board: *People who speak English think differently from people who speak ______.* Tell students to put their native language in the blank.
- Put students from different language groups in pairs (if possible) to discuss the sentence.
- Call on students to share their ideas with the class.

"Language shapes the way we think and determines what we think about."

Benjamin Lee Whorf
American linguist, (1897–1941)

Chapter Overview

Reading Selections

If We Could Talk with Animals…

"*Parentese*"

Reading Skills and Strategies

Previewing the topic and vocabulary

Previewing the reading

Identifying the main ideas

Identifying details

Getting meaning from context

Understanding italics and quotation marks

Skimming for main ideas

Critical-Thinking Skills

Categorizing

Interpreting a photograph

Identifying details and analyzing material using graphic organizers

Identifying inferences

Distinguishing facts from assumptions

Summarizing a paragraph

Vocabulary Building

Understanding words with multiple meanings

Focusing on the Academic Word List

Working with prefixes and suffixes

Understanding words in phrases

Learning new vocabulary: making a vocabulary log

Language Skills

Discussing the nature/nurture question

Writing a paragraph

Focus on Testing TOEFL® iBT

Focusing on comprehension questions about details

Vocabulary

Nouns
- brain
- capacity*
- chatter
- communication*
- creatures
- degree
- echoes
- gender*
- gestures
- glue
- grin
- journal*
- lexigrams
- mammals
- nature
- organs
- percent*
- pod
- prey
- primates
- research*
- species
- structures*
- subjects
- swagger

Verbs
- acquire*
- claims
- coin
- echo
- feeds
- focusing*
- reassure
- vocalize
- wagging

Adjective
- identical*

Adverb
- upright

Idioms and Expressions
- head (of something)
- head back
- picked up
- shedding light on

*These words are from the Academic Word List. For more information on this list, see www.victoria.ac.nz/lals/resources/ academicwordlist/.

If We Could Talk with Animals...

Before You Read

1 Previewing the Topic

- Have students look at the photos.
- Have them read the questions and write brief answers.
- Put students in small groups to practice asking and answering the questions.
- Call on students to share their answers with the class.

REPRODUCIBLE Expansion Activity

- The aim of this activity is for students to find out more about each other and begin thinking about the theme of this chapter.
- Photocopy and distribute **Black Line Master 17** "Find Someone Who..." on page BLM17 of this Teacher's Manual.
- Model the activity. Call on a student and ask: *Do you have a dog?* Continue asking until someone answers *yes*. Ask: *How does it communicate with you?* Listen to the answer. Point out that when students find someone who answers *yes*, they can write that person's name on the line.
- Have students walk around the room and ask questions until they write someone's name next to each item. Point out that they can use a classmates' name only once.
- When students complete the worksheet, ask each one to tell the class something he or she learned (*Ming has a bird, and it sings to her.*).

2 Previewing Vocabulary

- Read the directions to the students.
- Have them put a check (✓) next to the words they know.
- Remind them **not** to use a dictionary during this part of the lesson.
- Tell them to put the stress on words of more than one syllable as they listen to the audio.
- Write these words on the board as examples: *chat'ter, gen'der, swag'ger.*
- Start the audio.
- Have the students write the words on the board, marking the stress.

ANSWER KEY

Nouns
brain
chat'ter
crea'tures
degree'
ech'o
gen'der
ges'tures
grin
lex'igrams
mam'mals
or'gans
pod
prey
pri'mates
spe'cies
sub'jects
swag'ger

Verbs
acquire'
claims
coin
ech'oes
feeds
reassure'
vo'calize
wag'ging

Adverb
up'right

Idioms and Expressions
head (of something)
head back'
picked up'
shedding light' on

3 Previewing the Reading

- Put students in pairs to practice asking and answering the questions.
- Call on students to share their answers with the class. Their answers may vary.
- Write on the board a few of the questions they may have about the reading.

Read

4 Reading an Article

- On the board write *"How do animals communicate? Do animals have the capacity to learn language?"* and ask students to think about this question and the other questions you have written on the board as they are reading.
- Have the students read the passage silently within a time limit (10–15 minutes), or have them follow along as you play the audio.
- Tell them to underline any words or phrases that are new or that they don't understand. Remind them **not** to use a dictionary during this part of the lesson.
- Tell students to think about the questions on the board if they finish the reading quickly.
- Start the audio.
- When the time limit is reached or the audio is finished, point to the questions on the board and ask students if they found the answers.

Content Note

- Dr. Doolittle, a character invented by the British writer Hugh Lofting (1886–1947), was a veterinarian who could communicate with animals, even imaginary ones. Eddie Murphy made two comedy films based on this character in 1998 and 2001.
- Dr. Jane Goodall is a primatologist who has studied the behavior of chimpanzees in Tanzania, Africa, since 1960. She was the first to document that chimps used tools, hunted for meat, and had diverse personalities. She has taught and lectured about chimps all over the world.
- Dr. Con Slobodchikoff is a professor of biology at the University of Northern Arizona. He has studied colonies of prairie dogs and interpreted the alarm calls they use to protect the colony from predators.
- Dr. Louis Herman founded the Dolphin Institute at the Marine Mammal Laboratory of the University of Hawaii over 30 years ago. He studied these intelligent animals to learn more about their cognitive, behavioral, and sensory capabilities.
- Dr. Noam Chomsky has been a professor of linguistics at the Massachusetts Institute of Technology (MIT) for many decades. His seminal work, *Transformational Analysis*, changed the way linguists thought about grammar and speech.

After You Read

5 Getting the Main Ideas

- Read the directions and call on one student to read the first statement. Ask the class for the answer.
- Have the students continue with the rest of the statements individually. Students can check their answers with a partner if they finish quickly.
- Finish checking the answers as a class.

ANSWER KEY

1. T **2.** F **3.** F **4.** T **5.** F **6.** T **7.** F

6 Checking Your Understanding

Best Practice

Interacting with Others

These types of collaborative activities help students get a better understanding of the ideas in the reading passage through interacting with other students. They can clarify answers and reinforce knowledge with the assistance of their group members.

- Divide students into small groups for this activity. Read the directions.
- Tell students to work together by identifying the paragraphs in which the answers can be found and underlining the sentences.
- Circulate and help students if necessary.

ANSWER KEY

1. Animals communicate by using smell, body language, and vocalizations. [Subtitles of paragraphs B, C, and D]
2. Dolphins have been taught a language of hand symbols. [F] Chimps have been taught to understand and use American Sign Language (ASL) and symbols on a keyboard (lexigrams). [G]
3. Dogs wag their tails when they're happy and put their chest on the floor and rear end in the air when they want to play. Chimps swagger and wave their arms or throw branches when they're angry; they lower themselves to the ground and hold out their hands or show their rear ends when they're nervous in the presence of a more powerful chimp; a more powerful chimp touches, hugs, or kisses a nervous chimp to reassure her; when chimps are nervous or fearful, they "smile" by showing their teeth in a grin similar to one humans make. [C]
4. Biological evidence shows that an area of the brain in chimps, the *planum temporale*, is essentially identical to that of humans. [I]

7 Getting Meaning from Context

- On the board, put the phrase *Clues to Meaning*. Under it, write the following punctuations marks (words and symbols) and expressions:

  commas , ________ ,
  parentheses (________)
  dashes – ________ –

  in other words
  that is/*i.e.* (*id est* in Latin)

- Tell students to look for these punctuation marks and expressions when they see words or phrases they don't understand. These clues to meaning will help them understand new words and phrases.
- Read the directions and the first example.

ANSWER KEY

1. shedding light on 2. wagging
3. gestures 4. head back 5. upright
6. pod 7. grin 8. reassure 9. vocalize
10. prey 11. swagger 12. species 13. brain
14. claims 15. gender 16. mammals
17. acquire 18. chatter

8 Categorizing

- Read the directions.
- Give students a time limit (5 minutes). Check answers when they have finished.

ANSWER KEY

1. creatures 2. primates

FOCUS

Understanding Words with Multiple Meanings

- On the board, write the word *homophone* and the Greek roots: *homo* = *same* and *phone* = *sound*. Explain that it is a word that sounds the same, but with two or more different meanings. Sometimes homophones have the same spelling.
- Write these examples on the board and explain to students:

  The *chair* of the biology department sat in the most comfortable *chair*.

  The chimp found a *quarter* on the floor; then he ate a *quarter* of an apple.

- Call on students to read the examples in the book.

9 Understanding Words with Multiple Meanings

- Read the directions and have students do the activity.

ANSWER KEY

1. feeds **2.** degree **3.** head **4.** organs
5. subject **6.** pick up **7.** coin

FOCUS

Understanding Italics and Quotation Marks (Quotes)

Italics

Write these examples on the board for each bullet point and explain:

- Emphasis—*Most* dolphins can understand and follow hand signals.
- Meaning—*Syntax* distinguishes language from general communication.
- Title—The journal *Science* contains many interesting articles.
- Foreign word—The *planum temporale* in both humans and chimps is the same size.

Quotation Marks

Write these examples on the board for each bullet point and explain:

- Direct speech—When the chimp's kitten died, she signed, "Me sad."
- Something different, not literal meaning—What are honeybees "saying" when they dance?

10 Understanding Italics and Quotations

- Read the directions.
- Give the students a time limit (15 minutes).
- If students finish early, have them check their answers with a partner.

ANSWER KEY

B.

"Language"	something different
"smell-messages"	something different
"home"	something different

C.

"dance"	something different
"saying"	something different
"I want to play."	direct speech
"smiles"	something different

D.

"songs"	something different

E.

"talking"	something different
"say"	something different
"There's a tall blue human coming from the north."	direct speech

F.

(*ball, basket, pipe*)	meaning
(*big, small, red*)	meaning
(*left, right*)	meaning
(*go, take*)	meaning
(*in, under*)	meaning
"Go to the ball on your right and take it to the basket."	direct speech

H.

"take the potato outdoors"	direct speech
"go outdoors and get the potato"	direct speech
good, funny, hungry, stupid	meaning
"You me out."	direct speech
"Me banana you banana me you give."	direct speech
"water bird"	direct speech
"green banana"	direct speech
"Me sad."	direct speech

I.

"Lana tomorrow scare snake river monster"	direct speech
planum temporale	foreign language
Science	title
"essentially identical"	direct speech

J.

"Is it language?"	direct speech
syntax	meaning
"Some people think of language like pregnancy—you either have it or you don't."	direct speech
"a continuum of skills"	direct speech

11 Finding Details

Best Practice

Organizing Information

Activities such as this will teach students to organize information from a reading passage using a graphic organizer called a T-chart. This allows students to better assimilate and recall information at a later date, making it a valuable study tool. In this case, students identify examples of different types of animal communication mentioned in the passage.

- Direct students' attention to the T-chart. Ask them which animals use the types of communication listed in the first column.
- Tell them to work individually or in pairs to find information in the passage to fill in the second column. They can also do this assignment for homework.

ANSWER KEY

Answers may vary.

Types of Communication	Examples
smell	Smells have different meanings: to attract a mate, send a warning, mark a territory, or communicate where to find food.
body language	Body language can show directions to food or flowers, to express emotions or desires, or to demonstrate status.
vocalizations	Vocalizations can locate or identify objects or communicate with members of a group.
chatter (by prairie dogs)	Chatter can alert members of a group to danger or distinguish among creatures as to degree of danger.
symbols (used by dolphins)	Symbols like hand signals can be used to give commands to animals that they learn to follow.
symbols (used by primates)	Symbols like ASL and lexigrams can also be used for communication between chimps and humans.

12 Checking Your Vocabulary

- Read the directions to the students.
- Divide them into small groups and tell them to work on the **Previewing Vocabulary,** taking turns and following the directions. You may want to give them a time limit (10–15 minutes) for this activity.
- Remind them that they should **not** use a dictionary—unless you think that it is appropriate at this point in the lesson.
- Discuss any vocabulary items with which the students are still having difficulty.

13 Discussing the Reading

Best Practice

Making Use of Academic Content

Activities such as this will help students extract meaning from context, a skill necessary for academic success. Although they may understand the main ideas in the reading passage about animal communication, they may not understand whether or not this communication can be considered "language." Taking notes on important details will help them develop this skill.

- Remind the students of the question from the last paragraph: Do animals simply communicate or do they really have a language?
- Ask the students to raise their hands if they think that the following animals have a language: bees and ants, dogs and cats, dolphins, prairie dogs, chimpanzees.
- Direct their attention to the charts in items 1 and 2 and read the directions.
- Divide students into small groups and ask them to fill in the T-charts. Students' answers may differ from those listed here.

ANSWER KEY

Answers may vary.

1.

Communication	Language
Communication is the ability to use smell, body language, vocalizations, or symbols to relay messages to others of the same or different species.	Language is the ability to use vocalizations or symbols according to a set of rules, or *grammar*, that entails word order, or *syntax*. Mammals like dolphins and chimps may have a primitive ability to use language with training.

2.

Species	Capacity for language?	Evidence
prairie dogs	no	The chatter of prairie dogs seems to have as its main function to alert the colony to danger. Although they may be able to communicate 50 discrete meanings, we do not know if they use syntax.
dolphins	not sure	Although dolphins can understand and follow hand signals that have grammar and word order, they cannot, in turn, use these signals to communicate.
chimps	yes	Trained chimps can both understand and use ASL and lexigrams syntactically in short sentences and even coin new expressions when they don't know a word.

Expansion Activity

- The aim of this activity is for students to think further about animal communication by making the sounds animals make in their language. It's also fun, but if students don't feel comfortable doing it, they can sit and watch.
- Ask students from the same country to sit together in groups around the room.
- Ask each group to make the sound of one of the animals listed in the book.
- You might add other animals to the list, e.g., crow, sheep, goat, horse, camel, elephant, tiger, and so on.
- Discuss reasons for differences.

"Parentese"

Before You Read

1 Previewing the Topic

- Have students read the questions and write brief answers.
- Put students into single-sex pairs (i.e., women together and men together) to practice asking and answering questions. Give them a time limit (5–10 minutes) to finish the discussion.
- Call on students from each pair to share their answer with the class.

2 Identifying the Main Ideas

- Write these languages on the board and underline the last syllable: *Chin<u>ese</u>, Japan<u>ese</u>, Vietnam<u>ese</u>, Portugu<u>ese</u>*. Ask who speaks these languages. Explain that the reading is about another language, *parent<u>ese</u>*, and ask students to guess who speaks it.
- Read the directions and tell students to begin.
- Check the answers.

ANSWER KEY

A. (D) **B.** (B) **C.** (A) **D.** (A) **E.** (D)

Content Note

- Dr. Deborah Tannen is a professor of linguistics at Georgetown University in Washington, D.C. She has written many articles and books about gender differences in the speech of men and women.
- Emory University in Atlanta, Georgia, promotes studies in cognition and development in the department of psychology. Professors and graduate students do research on how both child and adult listeners interpret the different intentions, thoughts, and feelings of speakers.
- Dr. Campbell Leaper is a professor of psychology at the University of California at Santa Cruz. He has studied gender-related variations in parent-child speech.

After You Read

3 Getting Meaning from Context

- Read the directions.
- Remind students **not** to use a dictionary during this part of the lesson.
- Check the answers.

ANSWER KEY

Paragraph A

1. verbal

2. glue

Paragraph B

3. emotions

Paragraph C

4. realize

5. respond

6. apparently

Paragraph D

7. nature

8. nurture

9. evidence

4 Critical Thinking: Identifying Inferences

Best Practice

Cultivating Critical Thinking

Activities such as this will help students identify inferences from statements in the reading. Even though they may think that some of the statements are true, they must consider them in the light of the reading to determine if they are inferences.

- Read the directions.
- Point out the answer in the first item.
- Tell the students to use highlighters to find the phrases in the reading, if possible.
- Then have the students check the statements where they have found the phrases from which they inferred the information and then write them on the lines.
- Check the answers when students are done.

ANSWER KEY

Answers may vary.

Paragraph A

1. ✓ *Most people believe that women talk more… but this is a stereotype.*

2. ✓ … *women are more verbal—talk more—in private situations/men talk more in public situations.*

Paragraph B

4. ✓ *There is also far more talk about emotion, especially sadness, with daughters than with sons.*

Paragraph C

5. ✓ *It is a known fact that at birth, males are a little less developed than females are. They don't vocalize… and they don't have as much eye contact. Female babies vocalize, look at their parents…*

Paragraph D

7. ✓ *A toy grocery store naturally involves more conversation.*

8. ✓ *A boy gets a car he can take apart and put back together again.*

Paragraph E

9. ✓ *Both boys and girls need "task-oriented" toys such as take-apart cars. With these toys, they practice the language that they will need, as adults, in work situations. Both boys and girls also need "social, interactive" toys such as a grocery store. With these toys, they practice the kind of conversation that is necessary in relationships with friends and family.*

Strategy

Distinguishing Facts from Assumptions

- Write the "signal words" on the board:

  FACT: found proof a known fact evidence
  ASSUMPTION: believe apparently
  suggest seem may/might

- Call on a student to read the explanation from the **Strategy Box**.

5 Distinguishing Facts from Assumptions

- Read the directions and tell students to go back to the reading and underline the signal words for the fact or assumption.
- Then have the students write *fact* or *assumption* in the activity.
- Check answers.

ANSWER KEY

1. assumption: Most people **believe** that women talk more. [A]
2. fact: They **found evidence** that parents talk very differently… [B]
3. fact: It is **a known fact** that at birth… [C]
4. fact:… a study from UCSC **provides evidence** that… [D]
5. assumption:… Campbell Leaper… **believes** that the choice of toys is important. [E]
6. assumption: The **data suggest** that biology does not have to be… [E]

6 Discussing the Reading

- Direct the students' attention to the questions and read them.
- Divide students into small groups to discuss the answers and fill in the Venn diagram. Students' answers may differ from those listed here.

ANSWER KEY

Answers may vary.

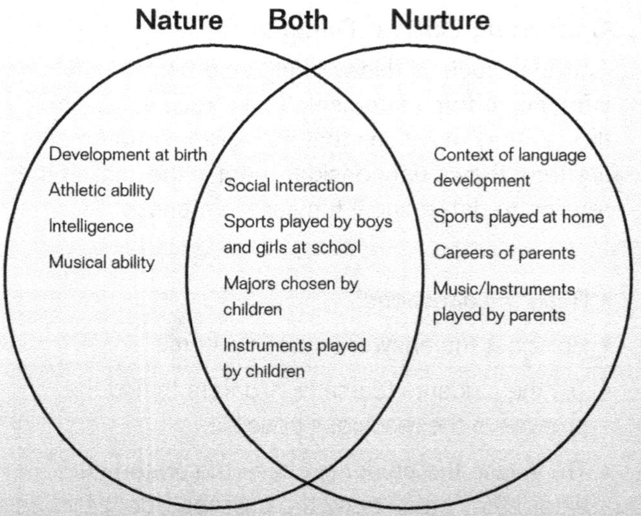

Responding in Writing

7 Summarizing

Best Practice

Scaffolding Instruction

Activities such as this will help students develop the ability to choose the main idea and important details of a paragraph in order to write a summary. By developing a model together, students are better equipped to write a summary independently later.

- Read the directions to the students. Write an outline of paragraph A on the board or on a transparency for an overhead projector (OHP):

  Men and women—different styles of communication

  Women—private situations = relationships
  Men—public situations = information, status
  Differences in childhood

  girls—best friend > talking; verbal skills
  boys—groups > doing; mathematics

- Write a summary of paragraph A on the board or a transparency:

  Men and women have very different styles of communication. Generally, women talk more in private situations and use conversation to form relationships. Men talk more in public situations and use conversation to give information or show status. Actually, these differences begin in childhood when girls play with their best friends and develop verbal skills. Boys, on the other hand, play in groups in which they do rather than say things. As a result, girls are usually better at languages, while boys are better at math.

- For variety, assign pairs of students a certain paragraph to outline and summarize.
- When students finish, have them compare their summary with those students who summarized the same paragraph.

8 Writing Your Own Ideas

- Read the directions to the students. You can assign the writing for homework or classwork.
- Be sure they identify the main idea of their paragraph.

Talk It Over

9 Toys

- For variety, visit a toy store nearby. Or bring in toy catalogs so students can cut out pictures and make posters in small groups that they can share with the class.

Reproducible Expansion Activity

- The aim of this activity is to further explore the theme of differences between male and female communication while children are playing.
- Make a list of toy websites or use the ones below.
- Check them before giving the assignment to students.
- Photocopy and distribute **Black Line Master 18** "Toys for Girls and Boys" on page BLM18 of this Teacher's Manual.
- Read the directions and the two examples.
- Divide the students into small groups.
- Give students a time limit (20–30 minutes) to do the activity. Alternatively, you can assign it for homework.
- When students complete the worksheet, tell them to present their toys to the class.

  http://www.adventuretoys.co.uk/
  http://www.toys.com/
  http://www.toysrus.com
  http://www.mastermindtoys.com/

1 Focusing on Words from the Academic Word List

- Direct students' attention to the list.
- Say the words and ask them to repeat, marking the stress on the appropriate syllable: *acquire', capa'city, communica'tion, fo'cusing, iden'tical, jour'nal, re'search, struc'tures, percent'.*
- Ask students to repeat the list of words by themselves.
- Tell them to put the words in the sentences.
- When they finish, have them check their answers on page 147, paragraph I.

ANSWER KEY

1. communication
2. capacity
3. acquire
4. research
5. focusing
6. structures
7. journal
8. identical
9. capacity
10. percent

FOCUS

Prefixes and Suffixes

- Direct students' attention to the list. Tell them you will read the prefixes and suffixes, and they will read the meanings aloud.

2 Working with Prefixes and Suffixes

- Read the directions. Call on a student to read the first example out loud.
- For variety, have students read in pairs or small groups.
- Tell them to begin the activity with their partners.

ANSWER KEY

1. converse (v) conversation (n) conversational (adj); conversation, converse, conversational
2. linguist (n) linguistic (adj) linguistics (n); linguistics, linguist, linguistic
3. reassurance (n) reassure (v) reassuringly (adv); reassure, reassurance, reassuringly
4. able (v) ability (n) ably (adv); ability, able, ably
5. appear (v) apparent (adj) apparently (adv); Apparently, apparent, appear
6. simple (adj) simplify (v) simplified (adj); simplify, simplified, simple
7. vocal (adj) vocalize (v) vocalization (n); vocalize, vocal, vocalization

3 Understanding Words in Phrases

- Write these phrases on the board and tell students that they always go together in this order: *black and white, come and go, up and down, back and forth.*
- Tell them there are many other phrases that are commonly used together in academic writing.
- Read the directions and let them begin the activity.

ANSWER KEY

Paragraph A

1. together **2.** gain **3.** out **4.** at

Paragraph B

5. light on

Paragraph C

6. known **7.** eye **8.** pay

Paragraph D

9. provide **10.** apart/back together **11.** on

Paragraph E

12. self-fulfilling

Strategy

Learning New Vocabulary: Making a Vocabulary Log

- On the board, copy the chart at the bottom of the **Strategy Box**. Explain the steps in making a Vocabulary Log.
- Write another word and elicit responses from the class: for example, *hybrid—a composite: The Toyota Prius is a hybrid car.*

4 Making a Vocabulary Log

- Tell students to choose five words from Chapters 1–7.
- Explain that using these five words, they should follow the steps from the **Strategy Box** to make their own Vocabulary Log.
- Tell students you will check their logs every week.

5 Searching the Internet

Best Practice

Activating Prior Knowledge

Activities such as this will enable students to link knowledge recently acquired with new information they gather from research. By working with partners, students will be able to think about what they have learned, add to it from what they encounter in their research, and share it with the rest of the class in a supportive environment.

- Divide students into pairs or small groups.
- Allow the groups to choose their topic. Instruct them to look at websites on the Internet; here are a few of them, but there are many more:

  Jane Goodall Institute
  http://www.janegoodall.org/

  Con Slobodchikoff
  http://conslobodchikoff.com/

  Louis Herman
  http://www.dolphin-institute.org/

  Deborah Tannen
  http://www9.georgetown.edu/faculty/tannend/

- Have the students present their findings to the class.

FOCUS TOEFL® iBT

Comprehension Questions About Details

- Read the instructions in the box or call on two students to do so.
- Tell them that in tests such as the TOEFL® iBT, they won't be able to read the questions before they start. However, they will see the paragraph that contains the answer to each question after they skim the passage.

1 Practice

- Tell students to read the questions on pages 166–167.
- Remind them to keep the questions in mind as they read the passage so they can mark the answers with a highlighter.
- Remind students **not** to use a dictionary during this part of the lesson.
- Give them a time limit (10 minutes).
- Check the answers.

ANSWER KEY

1. C **2.** A **3.** C **4.** D **5.** C **6.** C

Content Note

- Dr. Alan Firth was born and raised in England, but he got his Ph.D. and then became a professor at Aalborg University in northern Denmark. He has studied cross-cultural, business, and telecommunication interaction in English, and written numerous articles and books on those subjects.
- His Royal Highness, Prince Charles, the Prince of Wales, is heir apparent to the throne of the United Kingdom and the 15 Commonwealth Realms. He studied at Trinity College, Cambridge, and was the first member of the British Royal family to receive a degree. He also served in the British Royal Air Force and Royal Navy, as is the custom for male members of the royal family.
- Tom McArthur, an honorary fellow at the University of Exeter, wrote the *Oxford Companion to the English Language* and the *Oxford Guide to World English*. The latter book gives not only standard versions of British and American English, but also six geopolitical categories of English and its variations.
- The Australian government hosted the Cultural Diversity Conference in April, 1995, and well-known speakers from various sectors were invited to give papers. Dr. Braj Kachru, professor of linguistics at the University of Illinois, gave a talk titled the *International Nature of Modern English*, describing the *inner circle* of countries that speak it (USA—UK—Canada—Australia—New Zealand), the *outer circle* (Bangladesh—Ghana—India—Kenya—Malaysia—Nigeria—Pakistan—Philippines—Singapore—Sri Lanka—Tanzania—Zambia), and the *expanding circle* (China—Caribbean countries—Egypt—Indonesia—Israel—Japan—Korea—Nepal—Saudi Arabia—South Africa—South America—Taiwan—Commonwealth of Independent States [CIS]—Zimbabwe).

Beyond the Reading

2 Interviewing

- Read the directions.
- Students can choose to do one of these activities or the **Expansion Activity** with the Black Line Master.

REPRODUCIBLE

Expansion Activity

- The aim of this activity is to get students to think about the changes in the English language and the changes that are occurring in their own language because of the influence of English.
- Photocopy and distribute **Black Line Master 19** "Slang Expressions" on page BLM19 of this Teacher's Manual.
- Read the directions and do the first one together, writing the phrase on the board. If students have difficulty with Part I, do the rest with the class.
- Elicit an example for Part II (e.g., *biru* in Japanese is *beer* in English; *un parking* in Caribbean Spanish is *parking lot/garage*). Tell students to stand up and talk to others from their language group to finish the list, trying to think of a "pure" word from their language as a substitute.
- When students have completed the worksheet, have them put their words on the board in groups and present them to the class.

Self-Assessment Log

- Read the directions aloud and have students check vocabulary they learned in the chapter and are prepared to use.
- Have students check the strategies practiced in the chapter (or the degree to which they learned them). They have actually used all these strategies in Chapter 7.
- Put students in small groups. Ask students to find the information or an activity related to each strategy in the group.
- Tell students to find definitions in the chapter for any words they did not check.

CHAPTER 8

Tastes and Preferences

In this
CHAPTER

Students will read about the Silk Road and its history and significance in the first reading. They will also learn about the influence of religion on art and of the various civilizations that left their mark along the way of the caravans. In the second reading, students will learn about body art and the role it plays in the expression of cultural values and traditions. From clothing and decoration, to body and face paint, this form of art shows how ideal beauty among civilizations has differed through the ages.

Chapter Opener

- Direct students' attention to the photo. Then have students work in small groups to answer the questions in the Connecting to the Topic box. Go over the answers as a class.
- Read the quotation and ask students what it means.
- Put these words on the board: *ancient travel routes, caravans, trade, archaeology.*
- Divide students into small groups and ask them to discuss these words. Have them generate a list of words that they associate with these concepts.
- Elicit some of these words from the students and write them on the board.

"Science and art belong to the whole world, and before them vanish the barriers of nationality."

Johann Wolfgang von Goethe
German philosopher and writer
(1749–1832)

Chapter Overview

Reading Selections

The Silk Road: Art and Archaeology

Fashion: The Art of the Body

Reading Skills and Strategies

Previewing the topic and vocabulary

Previewing the reading

Getting meaning from context

Recognizing summaries in a reading

Identifying main ideas by analyzing details

Critical-Thinking Skills

Organizing information using an outline

Identifying and making inferences

Summarizing a paragraph

Vocabulary Building

Recognizing words with similar meanings

Understanding general and specific words

Understanding connotations

Focusing on the Academic Word List

Language Skills

Discussing ideas on art and beauty

Writing a paragraph

Focus on Testing TOEFL® iBT

Focusing on basic comprehension questions

Vocabulary

Nouns

- archaeologists
- architecture
- armor
- calligraphy
- caravan
- caves
- culture*
- destination
- documents*
- fabric
- frescoes
- mausoleums
- merchants
- mosques
- network
- oasis
- pitcher
- project*
- region*
- routes*
- silk
- spices
- statues
- technology*

Verbs

- called*
- decorated
- depict
- flower
- found*
- spread

Adjectives

- exquisite
- fertility
- holy
- significant*
- traditional*
- vast

Expression

- to this end

*These words are from the Academic Word List. For more information on this list, see www.victoria.ac.nz/lals/resources/ academicwordlist/.

The Silk Road: Art and Archaeology

Before You Read

1 Previewing the Topic

- Put students in small groups and have them discuss the questions.
- Call on students to share their answers with the class. Their answers may vary.
- Write on the board a few comments they may have about the discussion.

2 Previewing Vocabulary

- Read the directions to the students.
- Have them put a check (✓) next to the words they know.
- Tell them **not** to use a dictionary during this part of the lesson.
- Play the audio.

3 Previewing the Reading

- Read the questions and call on students to answer them.
- Comment on the answers, if necessary.

ANSWER KEY

Answers may vary.

1. Art and Archeology along the Silk road
2. Cross-Cultural Evidence; What Was the Silk Road?; Art, Religion, and the Silk Road; A Question of Time: Two Views; The Silk Road Today
3. The Silk Road was in Asia; many beautiful buildings, natural places, and artifacts can be found along the Silk Road.

Read

4 Reading the Article

- Read the directions.
- On the board write *What was the Silk Road? What can we learn about ancient life in this region from a study of the art and archaeology?* And ask students to think about these questions as they are reading.
- Have students read the passage silently within a time limit (10–15 minutes) or have them follow along silently as you play the audio.
- Tell them to underline any words or phrases that are new or that they don't understand. Remind them **not** to use a dictionary during this part of the lesson.
- Play the audio.

Content Notes

- C.E. = Common Era or Christian Era; 79 C.E. = 79 A.D.
- B.C.E. = Before Common Era or Before Christian Era; 50 B.C.E. = 50 B.C.

After You Read

5 Checking Your Understanding

Best Practice

Making Use of Academic Content

Activities such as this will help expand students' ability to locate information in an academic text. With practice, they will learn to find answers to questions about a reading quickly and accurately and discuss it with peers.

- Read the directions.
- Put students in small groups and have them answer the questions within a time limit (10–15 minutes).
- Call on different students to give the answers.
- Discuss further if necessary.

ANSWER KEY

1. The three pieces of evidence were:
   - a mirror from India with an ivory handle in the shape of a fertility goddess, found in the Roman city of Pompeii, destroyed by a volcano in 79 C.E.;
   - a water pitcher in the shape of a vase combining different styles from Persia, Central Asia, and Greece, found in the tomb of Li Xian, a Chinese military official who died in 569 C.E.;
   - thousands of objects from Vietnam, western China, Iraq, the Roman Empire, and Egypt were found in the 8th century Shosoin Treasure House in Nara, Japan.
2. The opposite ends of the Silk Road were East Asia and the Mediterranean.
3. The goods whose method of production was kept a secret were Chinese silk and Mediterranean glass.
4. Merchants moved many goods such as spices, musical instruments, tea, valuable stones, wool, linen, and other fabrics. Ideas and knowledge were also moved along the Silk Road.
5. Merchants moved goods along the Silk Road using caravans.
6. The evidence of the movement of Buddhism to China is in the paintings and statues left behind; in Dunhuang, China, Buddhists dug a series of caves with frescoes depicting religious scenes and daily life.
7. Islamic art and architecture flowered along the Silk Road; in Samarkand, Timur built mosques, mausoleums, and palaces decorated with arabesques and Arabic calligraphy.
8. In the Takla Makan Desert in Central Asia, tall people were found in tombs; they dressed in brightly colored wool and wore leather boots; they raised sheep and horses, used cowry shells for decoration, and ate bread, although wheat did not grow in that area.
9. Yo-Yo Ma's Silk Road Project encourages the preservation and spread of the living arts of these traditional lands.

6 Getting the Meaning from Context

- Read the directions. Remind students **not** to use a dictionary until they have completed this part of the lesson.
- Check the answers when students finish.

ANSWER KEY

1. verb/wall paintings/show, display
2. noun/built mosques/Islamic religious worship/places of worship in Islamic religion, buildings for Islamic religious activities

Strategy

Getting Meaning from Context

- Write the two sentences in the **Example** on the board.
- Have two students read them.
- Ask which words in the sentences give clues to the meaning of *tombs.*
- Underline the words *died* and *people's bodies.*
- Tell students when they don't know the meaning of a word to use the strategy of looking at several contexts when possible.

7 Getting Meaning from Context

- Read the directions. Remind students **not** to use a dictionary until they have completed this part of the lesson.
- Check the answers when students finish.

ANSWER KEY

1. "rooms" inside mountains
2. religious, sacred
3. incredible, beautiful

8 Checking Your Vocabulary

- Read the directions.
- Put students in small groups and have them find the answers.
- Give students a time limit (10–15 minutes).
- Call on different students to give the answers.
- Discuss further if necessary.

ANSWER KEY

1. archaeologists **2.** armor **3.** fabric
4. calligraphy **5.** oasis **6.** to this end
7. documents **8.** destination **9.** mausoleums
10. arabesques **11.** merchants **12.** flowered
13. significant

Strategy

Recognizing Summaries in a Reading

- Write the connecting words from the **Strategy Box** on the board.
- Read the directions and say the words, asking students to repeat after you.

9 Recognizing Summaries

- Read the directions.
- Have the students look back at the reading to find the answers.
- Check the answers when students finish.

ANSWER KEY

1. *Clearly*, long before the globalization of our modern world, trade was going on between very distant lands, and the objects tell a story about a place and time.
2. *In short*, the Silk Road was the way that goods and ideas moved across a vast area of Asia and southeastern Europe.
3. *In brief*, it is possible to follow the rise and fall of religions by studying the art and architecture along the Silk Road.
4. *Thus*, archaeologists are beginning to ask, "Were people moving along the Silk Road long before we had thought?"
5. *The result is* that the people along the ancient Silk Road continue to learn from each other.

10 Understanding Outlines

Best Practice

Organizing Information

Activities such as this will teach students to organize information by filling in an outline. This allows them to identify main ideas and supporting details from sections of text and put them into a format that facilitates review at a later date.

- Read the directions.
- Tell students to do the activity using the outline and put the subtopics in the right place.

ANSWER KEY

The Silk Road: Art and Archaeology

I. Introduction: Cross-Cultural Evidence
   A. *example: Indian mirror in Roman Pompeii*
   B. *example: pitcher with styles from three cultures in a Chinese tomb*

C. *example: the Shosoin Treasure House in Japan*

D. *trade between distant lands long before today's globalization*

II. What Was the Silk Road?

A. *series or network of trails that connect East Asia to the Mediterranean*

1. *exchange of goods (silk, glass, spices, etc.)*
2. *exchange of ideas and knowledge*

B. *two Silk Roads*

1. *literal*
2. *figurative*

III. Art, Religion, and the Silk Road

A. *the spread of Buddhism north and east from India*

B. *the spread of Islam toward the east*

IV. A Question of Time: Two Views

A. *historical view*

1. *100 B.C.E.*
2. *General Zhang Qian, sent by emperor*

B. *archaeological view*

1. *1000 B.C.E.*
2. *tombs in the Takla Makan Desert*

V. The Silk Road Today

A. *new technology*

B. *tourism*

C. *encouragement of living arts*

11 Checking Your Understanding

Best Practice

Scaffolding Instruction

Activities such as this will allow students to better understand a reading by scaffolding instruction. The information that they have just learned about the Silk Road can be used as a scaffold upon which they can integrate new information found during research.

- Write the two questions on the board:

  What was the Silk Road?

  What can we learn about ancient life in this region from a study of the art and archaeology?

- Have a short class discussion, asking students to elaborate on answers.

REPRODUCIBLE

Expansion Activity

- Photocopy and distribute **Black Line Master 20** "Traveling the Silk Road" on page BLM20 of this Teacher's Manual.
- Tell students in pairs or small groups to choose a region or country along the Silk Road and one of the products from the area that was transported along it.
- Keep a list to make sure that each one is different.
- Have students look on the Internet for information about the topic.
- Give them a few days to complete the assignment.
- If time permits, have them look for pictures (or draw them) and make a poster for their presentation and display in the classroom.
- When they finish, have them share their findings with the class.

12 Making Inferences

- Read the questions.
- Give the students five minutes to think about their answers to these questions.
- Call on different students to give the answers.

ANSWER KEY

1. Some were tall: a woman was 6 feet tall (1.83 meters), and a man 6 feet 6 inches (1.98 meters). Perhaps most astonishing, they had long noses and reddish hair, and the men wore beards.
2. People may have been traveling from Europe to Central Asia along the Silk Road as long ago as 1000 B.C.E. These people had characteristics of people from European countries rather than those from Asia.

13 Discussing the Reading

- Read the directions.
- Divide the students into small groups.
- Go around the room and listen to the discussion.
- Ask students to share their ideas with the class. (Answers will vary.)

Fashion: The Art of the Body

Before You Read

Strategy

Identifying Main Ideas by Analyzing Details

- Read the directions.
- Have a student read the paragraph in the example.
- Ask students what the different groups mentioned in the paragraph wear:

  the Inuit, nomadic desert people, the Indians of southern Chile, the tribal people of Australia.
- Ask students what the main idea is.

1 Identifying the Topic and Main Idea

- Read the directions.
- Remind students **not** to use a dictionary during this part of the lesson.
- Check the answers when students finish.

ANSWER KEY

Paragraph A	**1.** D	**2.** A, C, D	**3.** C
Paragraph B	**1.** D	**2.** A, B, D	**3.** B
Paragraph C	**1.** D	**2.** B, C	**3.** A
Paragraph D	**1.** C	**2.** B, C, D	**3.** B
Paragraph E	**1.** A	**2.** A, B, C	**3.** C

After You Read

2 Critical Thinking: Identifying Inferences

- Read the directions.
- Point out the answers in the first two examples.
- Tell the students to use highlighters to mark the phrases in the reading, if possible.
- Then have the students check the statements where they have found the phrases from which they inferred the information and then write them on the lines.
- Tell the students to work as quickly as possible.
- Check the answers when students finish.

ANSWER KEY

1. _✗_ All people wear clothing to keep warm.

2. _✓_ Fur provides warmth, while long, loose clothing is useful in hot weather.

The Inuit (Eskimos) wear animal fur to protect them against the cold winter weather. Nomadic desert people wear long, loose clothing for protection against the sun and wind of the Sahara.

3. _✗_ Rich people wear more clothing than poor people do.

4. _✓_ Social status might be less important now than it was in the past.

With the exception of the military, the divisions between different classes of society are becoming less clear. The clientele of a Paris café, for example, might include both working-class people and members of the highest society, but how can one tell the difference when everyone is wearing denim jeans?

5. _✗_ Some methods of body beautification may be uncomfortable or painful.

6. ✓ Body or face paint may make people feel protected.

Anthropologists explain that it is a form of magic protection against the dangers of the world outside the village, where men have to go for the hunt or for war.

7. ✗ Women are more interested than men in looking good.

8. ✓ There are some similarities between tribal people and modern urban people in their views of body decoration.

In modern societies, however, cosmetics are used mostly by women, who often feel naked, unclothed, without makeup when out in public—like a tribal hunter without his warpaint.

3 Discussing the Reading

- Put students in small groups to discuss the questions.
- Call on some groups to share their answers with the class and discuss.

Responding in Writing

4 Summarizing

- Read the directions. Tell students to choose one paragraph from paragraphs B, F, or G on pages 172–174.
- Give students a minute to decide which paragraph they will write about.
- Ask students who are going to summarize the same paragraph to sit together.
- Have them write a summary alone and then compare it to that of another student.
- When they have compared their summaries, collect and check them.

5 Writing Your Own Ideas

Best Practice

Activating Prior Knowledge

Activities such as summarizing a topic and expressing an opinion about it allow students to activate prior knowledge. This activity enables students to use their prior knowledge about society's views on these topics, formulate their own opinion, and express it in a letter to their teacher.

- Read the directions.
- Have students choose one of the topics listed and write you a letter for homework.
- Write this format on the board and tell students to copy it:

2/18/08

Dear ________,

I'd like to tell you my opinion of ________. In my country, many people think that ________ is ________. But I think that it is ________ because ________. In addition, ________________________________. In short, ________________________________.

Your student,

Abdul

- The next day, collect the letters.
- Pass them around to different students in the class. Make sure no one gets his or her own letter.
- Tell the students to read them and write the main idea of each letter at the bottom.
- Then have the students write a response to the letter on the back of the paper, telling their opinion on the topic.
- When students finish, they can give the letters back to the person who wrote them.
- After they have read them, collect and check them.

Talk It Over

6 Art and Beauty

- Read the directions.
- Divide students into small groups to discuss the questions about the quotations.
- Go around the room and listen to the discussions. Help the students with quotations they don't understand.
- Have them share their answers with the class.

7 Analyzing Advertisements

Best Practice

Cultivating Critical Thinking

Activities such as this allow students to engage in critical thinking as they consider the variety of beauty treatments available today. By doing research on the Internet and finding out how the treatment is done, by whom, and to whom, they will be better able to evaluate its worth and formulate an opinion about it.

- Ask students what kinds of beauty treatments are available to people today.
- Make a list on the board, dividing the treatments into categories, such as hair, skin, nails, body-building/slimming, injections (Botox, collagen), cosmetic surgery, and so on.
- Tell students to choose one of these categories to research and present to the class.

REPRODUCIBLE

Expansion Activity

- Photocopy and distribute **Black Line Master 21** "Beauty Treatments" on page BLM21 of this Teacher's Manual.
- Allow students to choose a type of beauty treatment in pairs or small groups.
- Have them go to the computer lab or do the activity at home.
- Give them a few days to finish the assignment.
- Tell students to make a poster or PowerPoint presentation of their research.
- Have them present their findings to the class.

Strategy

Recognizing Words with Similar Meanings

- Write the **Examples** from the **Strategy Box** on the board.
- Ask a student to read them.
- Elicit the meanings of the words (*course*, *class*, *lesson*) from the students, or read them to the students.

1 Recognizing Words with Similar Meanings

- Read the directions.
- Ask students to do the activity quickly.
- Check the answers with the class.

ANSWER KEY

1. b, c, a **2.** a, b, c **3.** c, a, b

Strategy

Understanding General and Specific Words

- Put the **Example** on the board:

  Beautiful art can be found in different kinds of structures: churches, mosques, and palaces.

- Underline the general word, *structures*, and the specific words, *churches*, *mosques*, and *palaces*.
- Ask students which word is general, and which words are specific.
- Tell them that the general word is the *category* that the particular words belong to.

2 Understanding General and Specific Words

- Read the directions.
- Ask students to do the activity quickly.
- Check the answers with the class.

ANSWER KEY

1. art **2.** writing **3.** architecture **4.** traveler **5.** transportation **6.** cosmetics **7.** music **8.** crime

Strategy

Understanding Connotations

- Write the **Examples** from the Strategy Box on the board.
- Ask a student to read them.
- Elicit the meanings of the words (*plump*, *large*, *fat*) from the students, or read them to the students.

3 Understanding Connotations

- Read the directions.
- Have students work on the activity in pairs.
- Check the answers when finished.

ANSWER KEY

1. + **2.** – **3.** – **4.** + **5.** – **6.** –

(3) plump (4) chubby

1. beautiful **2.** hideous **3.** gorgeous **4.** ugly **5.** beautiful **6.** ugly

4 Choosing the Appropriate Words

- Read the directions.
- Have students work on the activity in pairs.
- Check the answers when finished.

ANSWER KEY

1. B, C **2.** A, D **3.** C, D

5 Writing Words with Similar Meanings

Best Practice

Interacting with Others
Activities such as this will encourage students to expand their basic vocabulary and add variety to their speaking and writing. Making lists of words with similar meanings, or synonyms, on the board with other students will increase the range of their vocabulary and help them on the TOEFL® iBT.

- Read the directions.
- Have students work on the activity in pairs.
- Tell them to make lists of synonyms on the board.
- Discuss the differences in meaning, connotation, and usage with the class.

ANSWER KEY

Answers may vary.

1. adult female, mother
2. robber, burglar
3. speak, discuss, converse
4. think, know, hope
5. ancient, elderly, worn
6. tiny, petite, minuscule

6 Recognizing Words in Phrases

- Read the directions.
- Tell students to guess the words before they look them up.
- Have them check their answers with the reading.

[A] in the shape of...
[B] a network of...
[C] was used from... to...
[D] from... to...
[E] a desert oasis
[F] **1.** contributed to; **2.** In brief...
[H] To this end...

7 Focusing on Words from the Academic Word List

- Read the directions.
- Tell students to guess the words before they look them up.
- Have them check their answers with the reading on pages 174–175.

ANSWER KEY

1. culture **2.** technology **3.** routes
4. culture **5.** region **6.** founded
7. Project **8.** traditional **9.** continue

8 Searching the Internet

- Read the directions.
- Tell students to choose one of the topics.
- Divide the students into pairs or small groups according to the topic they have chosen.
- Tell them to find a website and prepare a short report.
- Have each person write, draw, or upload images for the presentation (PowerPoint, poster, drawings on board).
- Have them share their findings with the class.

FOCUS TOEFL® iBT

Questions About Basic Comprehension

- Put the three types of questions from **Chapter 1** on the board:

  Information questions—scanning for words or numbers

  Basic comprehension questions—vocabulary, grammar, organization of passage

  Reading to learn—main ideas, implied ideas, author's attitudes, relations among facts
- Explain the types of questions and read the paragraph in the box to students.
- Tell the students that they will do an activity that will help prepare them for the iBT.

1 Practice

- Read the directions, telling students to skim the reading on pages 164–165 of Chapter 7 in 5 minutes, as they have already read it before. Write the beginning and ending time on the board (e.g., 10:45–10:50).
- When time is up, tell them to do the questions in 5 minutes, and write the beginning and ending time on the board.
- Check the answers when students finish.

ANSWER KEY

1. A **2.** C **3.** A **4.** B **5.** C

Self-Assessment Log

- Read the directions aloud and have students check vocabulary they learned in the chapter and are prepared to use.
- Have students check the strategies practiced in the chapter (or the degree to which they learned them). They have actually used all these strategies in Chapter 8.
- Put students in small groups. Ask students to find the information or an activity related to each strategy in the group.
- Tell students to find definitions in the chapter for any words they did not check.

REPRODUCIBLE

Expansion Activity

- Photocopy and distribute **Black Line Master 22** "Spelling and Synonyms" on page BLM22 of this Teacher's Manual.
- Read the directions.
- Dictate the words from the **Target Vocabulary List** to the students if time is limited. Or write each word on a slip of paper and divide the slips among the students.
- Have each student say the word on the slip loudly and clearly to the class.
- Students write down 15 words on the **Black Line Master**.
- When all the words have been said, tell the students to write a synonym or meaning beside the word without using a dictionary.
- Have students check their own papers by looking at the **Target Vocabulary List** on page 195.
- When they finish, elicit synonyms or meanings. Students can use this sheet to study for the **Chapter Test**.

CHAPTER 9

New Frontiers

In this
CHAPTER

Students will read about the different parts of the brain and their functions. They will also learn about the teen brain, differences between male and female brains, and activities that can either damage or enhance the functioning of the brain. In the second reading, students will read about the familiar nature versus nurture controversy. Twin studies, genetics, and chemicals that stimulate or suppress the brain will also be explored in this regard.

"If the brain were so simple [that] we could understand it, we would be so simple [that] we couldn't."

Lyall Watson
African biologist
and author (1939–)

Chapter Opener

- Direct students' attention to the photo. Then have students work in small groups to answer the questions in the Connecting to the Topic box. Go over the answers as a class.
- Read the quotation and ask students what it means. Ask them if they know anything about Lyall Watson, and have them research some information about him.

Chapter Overview

Reading Selections

The Human Brain—New Discoveries

Personality: Nature or Nurture?

Reading Skills and Strategies

Previewing the topic and vocabulary

Previewing the reading

Predicting content of a reading

Identifying the main ideas and analyzing details

Skimming for main ideas

Critical-Thinking Skills

Analyzing diagrams and photographs

Distinguishing facts from assumptions

Synthesizing and applying information from a reading

Categorizing

Making inferences

Summarizing a paragraph

Vocabulary Building

Matching words with similar meanings

Putting words into categories

Analyzing word roots and affixes

Focusing on the Academic Word List

Language Skills

Expressing opinions based on facts

Identifying similarities and differences among family members

Writing a paragraph

Focus on Testing TOEFL® iBT

Getting meaning from context

Vocabulary

Nouns
- adults*
- blood vessels
- colleagues*
- evidence*
- hemispheres
- insights*
- institute*
- intelligence*
- intuition
- logic*
- maturation*
- maturity*
- memory
- neuroscientists
- origin
- researchers*
- toxins
- wiring

Verbs
- imply*
- rotate

Adjectives
- cognitive
- exposed*
- involved*
- logical*
- mature*
- mental*
- precise*
- repressed
- traditional*

Expression
- going into training

*These words are from the Academic Word List. For more information on this list, see www.victoria.ac.nz/lals/resources/ academicwordlist/.

The Human Brain—New Discoveries

Before You Read

1 Getting Started

Best Practice

Scaffolding Instruction
Activities such as this will allow students to better understand a reading by scaffolding instruction. The information that they learn from the drawing can be used as a scaffold upon which they can integrate new information from the reading.

- Direct students' attention to the drawing and have students say the name of each part of the brain after you. Ask them to read the captions about the brain.
- Put students in small groups and have them discuss the questions.
- Call on students to share their answers with the class. Their answers may vary.
- Write on the board a few of their comments.

ANSWER KEY

Answers may vary.

1. Compose music—cerebrum, cortex, temporal lobe, frontal lobe; throw a ball—cerebellum, occipital lobe, parietal lobe, frontal lobe; paint a picture—cerebrum, cortex, occipital lobe, parietal lobe, frontal lobe, cerebellum.
2. Cold—hypothalamus, cerebrum, cortex
3. Sunset—occipital lobe, cerebrum, cortex, temporal lobe, hypothalamus; tennis game—cerebrum, cortex, cerebellum
4. Man—occipital lobe, parietal lobe, cerebrum, cortex, frontal lobe, temporal lobe, hypothalamus; other answers will vary.
5. Answers will vary.

2 Previewing the Reading

- Read the questions and call on students to answer them.
- Comment on the answers, if necessary.

ANSWER KEY

1. The Human Brain—New Discoveries
2. Left Brain/Right Brain: Creativity; Memory—True or False?; The Teen Brain; Differences in Male and Female Brains; A Change of Mind?
3. Answers may vary.

3 Preparing to Read

- Read the directions.
- Call on different students to read each question.
- Ask students if they think the reading will answer that question.
- Comment on the answers, if necessary.

ANSWER KEY

Answers may vary.

1. ✓ **2.** ✓ **3.** ✓ **4.** ✓ **5.** – **6.** ✓ **7.** ✓
8. ✓ **9.** – **10.** ✓ **11.** –

4 Previewing Vocabulary

- Read the directions to the students.
- Have them put a check (✓) next to the words they know.
- Tell them **not** to use a dictionary during this part of the lesson.
- Play the audio.

Read

5 Reading an Article

- Read the directions.
- Have students read the passage silently within a time limit (10–15 minutes) or have them follow along silently as you play the audio.
- Tell them to underline any words or phrases that are new or that they don't understand. Remind them **not** to use a dictionary during this part of the lesson.
- Play the audio.

After You Read

6 Getting the Main Ideas

- Read the directions.
- Have students work on the activity individually.
- Call on different students to read the statements and give the answers.
- Discuss further if necessary.

ANSWER KEY

1. T **2.** T **3.** F **4.** F **5.** F **6.** T

7 Vocabulary Check

- Read the directions.
- Put students in pairs and remind them **not** to use a dictionary until they have completed this part of the lesson.
- Discuss the answers when students finish.

Strategy

Distinguishing Facts from Assumptions

- Write these words on the board:

  FACT information proven to be true

  ASSUMPTION ideas believed but not proven to be true

- Read the directions for the first part and tell the class to repeat the words after you and say the parts of speech:

certain adj.	objective adj.	scientific adj.
clear adj.	positive adj.	show v.
know v.	prove v.	sure adj.

- Read the directions for the second part and tell the class to repeat the words after you and say the parts of speech:

claim	possibly
(dis)agree	probably
doubt	subjective
imply	theorize
likely	think
possible	

8 Distinguishing Facts from Assumptions

- Read the directions.
- Tell students to do the activity in pairs.
- Check the answers when students finish.

ANSWER KEY

1. **fact**—*Psychologists agree that most of us have creative ability that is greater than what we use in daily life.*
2. **assumption**—*Therefore, many of us might not "exercise" our right hemisphere much, except through dreams, symbols, and those wonderful insights in which we suddenly find the answer to a problem that has been bothering us.*
3. **assumption**—*Can we be taught to use our right hemisphere more? Many experts believe so.*
4. **assumption**—*Classes at some schools and books (such as* The Inner Game of Tennis *and* Drawing on the Right Side of the Brain*) claim to help people "silence" the left hemisphere and give the right a chance to work.*
5. **fact**—*In fact, over 700 cases have been filed that are based on these repressed memories.*
6. **assumption**—*However, studies in the 1990s suggested that many of these might be false memories.*
7. **fact**—*It is known that small pieces of a memory (sound, sight, feeling, and so on) are kept in different parts of the brain; the limbic system, in the middle of the brain, pulls these pieces together into one complete memory.*
8. **fact**—*But it's certain that people can "remember" things that have never happened.*
9. **assumption**—*Most frightening, according to Dr. Michael Nash of the University of Tennessee, is that "there may be no structural difference" in the brain between a false memory and a true one.*
10. **fact**—*However, very recent studies provide evidence that the brain of a teenager differs from that of both children and adults.*
11. **assumption**—*Because, it is believed, the corpus callosum is involved in self-awareness and intelligence, the new studies imply that teens may not be as fully self-aware or as intelligent as they will be later.*
12. **fact**—*One recent study shows that there is a region in the hypothalamus that is larger in heterosexual men than it is in women and homosexual men.*
13. **assumption**—*The corpus callosum is larger in women than in men. This might explain the mystery of "female intuition," which is supposed to give women greater ability to "read" and understand emotional clues.*
14. **fact**—*a study from the University of Aberdeen and the University of Edinburgh, in England concludes that smoking makes people less intelligent.*
15. **assumption**—*meditation seems to change the "wiring" in the brain in several positive ways.*

9 Checking Your Understanding

Best Practice

Making Use of Academic Content

Activities such as this will help expand students' ability to locate information in an academic text. With practice, they will learn to find answers to questions about a reading quickly and accurately.

- Read the directions.
- Tell students to do the activity in pairs. Give them a time limit (10–15 minutes).
- Call on different students to read the questions and answers.
- Discuss further if necessary.

ANSWER KEY

Answers may vary.

1. Different parts of the brain are responsible for different functions of the body.
2. Animal brains have a subcortex, which is responsible for basic functions whereas human brains have the neocortex, which is where complex activities take place.
3. Some people use the right hemisphere more than others do.
4. The left side of the brain is where reading, writing, and mathematics are processed; the right side is where music, art, dreams, symbols, and insights are processed.
5. Not answered in the reading.
6. Yes, because small pieces of memory are kept in different parts of the brain, and the limbic system pulls these pieces together into one complete memory, making it possible to have a false one.
7. Meditation can improve our memories.
8. In teenagers' brains, the corpus callosum continues to grow, so the self-awareness and intelligence of young people are still developing.
9. Not answered in the reading.
10. Smoking and "infomania" can reduce intelligence.
11. Not answered in the reading.

10 Critical Thinking: Application

- Read the directions.
- Put students in small groups.
- Go around the room and comment on lists, if necessary.
- Ask students to share their lists with the class.

REPRODUCIBLE

Expansion Activity

- The aim of this activity is to encourage students to apply what they have learned in the reading to their own experience.
- Photocopy and distribute **Black Line Master 23** "Improving Your Brain" on page BLM23 of this Teacher's Manual.
- Put students in pairs or small groups to review paragraphs [H] and [I] and list things that are good and bad for the brain.
- Tell them to search the Internet and look for more ideas.
- Point out to students that they should also list how they plan to improve the functioning of their own brains.
- Give them a few days to complete the assignment.
- When they finish, have them share their findings with the class.

Personality: Nature or Nurture?

Before You Read

1 Identifying the Main Idea by Analyzing Details

- Read the directions.
- Remind students **not** to use a dictionary during this part of the lesson.
- Have students read the passage silently within a time limit (10–15 minutes) or have them follow along silently as you play the audio.
- Check the answers when students finish.

ANSWER KEY

A. **1.** D **2.** B, C, D, E
3. both nature and nurture play a role in determining a person's identity

B. **1.** C **2.** B, C, E
3. genetics (nature/biology) plays a significant role in determining personal characteristics and behavior

C. **1.** E **2.** A, B, C, E
3. a surprising number of traits are heritable, or due to nature

D. **1.** B **2.** A, C, D, E
3. genes work together with the chemicals in the body to influence personality

E. **1.** A **2.** A, B, D, E
3. although personality traits are largely heritable, the environment still plays an important role in their development

After You Read

2 Critical Thinking: Making Inferences

- Read the directions.
- Tell the students to work as quickly as possible.
- Check the answers when students finish.

ANSWER KEY

1. ✓ The philosophical question of nature/nurture is an old one.

The nature/nurture question is not a new one.

2. ✗ The environment in which Jim Springer and Jim Lewis grew up had no effect on their behavior or personality.

3. ✓ The goal of twin studies is to identify the amount of influence from genes and the amount from education and experiences that determine our identity.

Today, we realize that both play a role. The question now is, to what degree? To answer this question, researchers are studying identical twins, especially those who grew up in different environments.

Various research centers are studying identical twins in order to discover the "heritablility" of behavioral characteristics—that is, the degree to which a trait is due to genes ("nature") instead of environment.

4. ✓ The possibility of being happy is mostly a result of our genes, not our situations in life.

Another study tells us that happiness does not depend much on money or love or professional success; instead, it is 80 percent heritable!

5. ✗ A single gene determines each personality characteristic.

6. ✓ The genetic contribution to personality is complicated.

However, one gene alone cannot cause people to become anxious or homosexual or thrill seeking. Instead, many genes work together, and they direct the combination of chemicals in the body.

7. ✗ Human beings are able to change their genetics.

3 Discussing the Reading

- Read the directions.
- Put students in small groups to discuss the questions.
- Go around the room and comment on answers, if necessary.

Responding in Writing

4 Summarizing

- Read the directions.
- Give students a minute to decide which part they will write about.
- Ask students who are going to summarize the same paragraph to sit together.
- Have them write a summary alone and then compare it to that of one of the other students who is summarizing the same paragraph.
- When they have compared their summaries, collect and check them.

5 Writing Your Own Ideas

Best Practice

Activating Prior Knowledge
Activities such as applying a concept from a reading to their personal experience will help students understand it better. Writing a letter to a family member will enable them to explore a topic and perhaps come to a better understanding of it.

- Read the directions.
- Have students choose one of the topics listed and write a letter for homework.
- Write this format on the board and tell students to copy it:

4/25/07

Dear ________ ,

I remember when we used to talk about the vacation we spent in Ibiza when we were little. You said we stayed at a small hotel, but I remember that we camped out on the beach. We fished and ate what we caught, but you remember eating in country restaurants on the hillsides. We had a lot of fun on that vacation, but why do we each remember it so differently?

Your sister,
Anna

- The next day, collect the letters.
- Pass them around to different students in the class. Make sure no one gets his or her own letter.
- Tell the students to read them and write the main idea of each letter at the bottom.
- Then have the students write a response to the letter on the back of the paper, telling their opinion on the topic.
- When students finish, they can give the letters back to the person who wrote them.
- After they have read them, collect and check them.

Talk It Over

6 Genes for Crime?

Best Practice

Cultivating Critical Thinking
Activities such as this allow students to engage in critical thinking as they consider the possibility of the existence of a genetic link to violence or criminality. By also doing research on the Internet and investigating the details, they will be better able to evaluate the possibility and form an opinion about it.

- Have two students read the two paragraphs.
- Ask students what they think.
- Tell them they will research the topic in the next activity.

REPRODUCIBLE

Expansion Activity

- The aim of this activity is to engage the students in critical thinking about a topic related to the reading.
- Photocopy and distribute **Black Line Master 24** "Violence and Genetics" on page BLM24 of this Teacher's Manual.
- Tell students to outline the article according to the sections on the **Black Line Master**, if possible. They can also make up different sections.
- Have students go to the computer lab or do the activity at home.
- Give them a few days to finish the assignment.
- Allow students to choose sides on this issue after they do research and hold a debate.
- Have them present their findings to the class.

1 Understanding Words with Similar Meanings

- Read the directions.
- Ask students to do the activity quickly.
- Check the answers with the class.

ANSWER KEY

1. c, a, b **2.** b, a, c **3.** c, b, a **4.** c, a, b

Strategy

Putting Words in Categories

- Write the words from the **Example** in the **Strategy Box** on the board:

  laboratory, neuroscientist, subjects, experiment
- Ask a student to read them.
- Elicit the content area from the students (*science*).
- Read the explanation.

2 Putting Words in Categories

Best Practice

Organizing Information

Activities such as this will teach students to organize words into categories or content areas. This will help them in both reading and writing to recognize and use synonyms, distinguishing between slight differences in meaning.

- Read the directions.
- Have students work on the activity as a class.
- Check the answers when finished.

ANSWER KEY

1. ~~nurture~~ / genetics
2. ~~maturity~~ / young child
3. ~~musician~~ / medical/health
4. ~~creativity~~ / parts of the brain
5. ~~meditation~~ / illness, disorder, condition
6. ~~anxiety~~ / physical characteristics
7. ~~dreams~~ / subjects

FOCUS

Analyzing Word Roots and Affixes

- Read the directions.
- Read the **Affixes** and ask students to read the **Meanings**.

3 Analyzing Word Roots and Affixes

- Read the directions.
- Have students do the activity quickly.
- Check the answers.

ANSWER KEY

1. c **2.** a **3.** b **4.** e **5.** d **6.** a **7.** d

4 Focusing on Words from the Academic Word List

- Read the directions.
- Have students do the activity quickly.
- Check the answers.

ANSWER KEY

1. traditional **2.** mature **3.** evidence
4. Institute **5.** Mental **6.** maturation
7. colleagues **8.** involved **9.** intelligence
10. imply **11.** intelligent **12.** researchers
13. adults

5 Searching the Internet

Best Practice

Interacting with Others

Activities such as this will encourage students to explore a topic of interest with their peers. They will develop the skills of working together to find information and organizing it in a logical way to present it to the class.

- The purpose of this activity is to encourage students to do research on topics presented in the readings.
- Allow them to choose a topic and search the Internet with others who have chosen the same one.
- Have them prepare a poster or an outline on the board and present their topic to the class.
- Remind students that each one in the group must speak during the presentation.
- Have the other students write down one or two questions to ask the group after their presentation.

FOCUS TOEFL® iBT

Getting Meaning from Context

- Put these hints on the board:

A word can be defined or explained in

same	→	sentence
previous	→	*or*
following	→	a different paragraph

- Use the context to figure it out.
- Tell the students that the **Practice** will help prepare them for the iBT.

1 Practice

- Read the directions, telling students to do the activity quickly. Write a beginning and ending time on the board (10–15 minutes).
- When time is up, tell them to stop working.
- Check the answers when students finish.

ANSWER KEY

1. C **2.** D **3.** B **4.** C **5.** D **6.** C **7.** A

Self-Assessment Log

- Read the directions aloud and have students check vocabulary they learned in the chapter and are prepared to use.
- Have students check the strategies practiced in the chapter (or the degree to which they learned them). They have actually used all these strategies in Chapter 9.
- Put students in small groups. Ask students to find the information or an activity related to each strategy in the group.
- Tell students to find definitions in the chapter for any words they did not check.

REPRODUCIBLE

Expansion Activity

- The aim of this activity is to have students practice the parts of speech of words in the **Target Vocabulary**.
- Photocopy and distribute **Black Line Master 25** "Parts of Speech" on page BLM25 of this Teacher's Manual.
- Read the directions.
- Tell students to work individually and then in pairs.
- Have students check their work using a dictionary.

CHAPTER 10

Ceremonies

In this CHAPTER

Students will read about the different rites of passage and what they signify. Among the rites they will learn about are the passage to adulthood among Native Americans, the birth of a baby in Korea, Islamic weddings, and funerals in Thailand. They will also read a passage describing how some of these traditional rituals are changing as people seek to adopt those of other cultures. Finally, they will read about learning to drive in the United States, a rite of passage from adolescence to adulthood.

"When humans participate in ceremony, they enter a sacred space. Everything outside of that space shrivels in importance. Time takes on a different dimension."

Sun Bear
Medicine Chief of the Bear Tribe
Medicine Society (1929–1992)

Chapter Opener

- Direct students' attention to the photo. Then have students work in small groups to answer the questions in the Connecting to the Topic box. Go over the answers as a class.
- Read the quotation and ask students what it means. Ask them what they know about Sun Bear, or have them research his life.

Chapter Overview

Reading Selections

Rites of Passage

New Days, New Ways: Changing Rites of Passage

Reading Skills and Strategies

Previewing the topic and vocabulary

Previewing the reading

Identifying the main ideas and writing summaries of each paragraph in a reading

Understanding chronology: scanning for time words

Understanding symbols

Critical-Thinking Skills

Making inferences

Comparing and contrasting

Using a graphic organizer to organize and analyze information

Distinguishing facts from opinions

Summarizing a whole reading

Vocabulary Building

Determining categories

Analyzing word roots and affixes

Focusing on the Academic Word List

Language Skills

Applying information in the reading to personal situations

Conducting a survey on traditional and nontraditional weddings

Writing a paragraph

Focus on Testing TOEFL® iBT

Identifying main idea patterns

Vocabulary

Nouns
- bride
- coffin
- coming-of-age
- community*
- cremation
- deceased
- delivery
- funerals
- groom
- guidance
- incorporation*
- monks
- negotiations
- pregnancy
- proposal
- pyre
- rite of passage
- ritual
- scriptures
- status*
- taboos
- transition*
- trousseau
- vision*
- vision quest

Verbs
- chant
- regain
- vary*

Adjectives
- indigenous
- nomadic
- previous*

Adverb
- physically*

Expression
- ask for (a woman's) hand

*These words are from the Academic Word List. For more information on this list, see www.vuw.ac.nz/lals/research/academicwordlist/.

Rites of Passage

Before You Read

1 Getting Started

- Direct students' attention to the questions.
- Put students in small groups and have them discuss the questions.
- Call on students to share their answers with the class. Their answers may vary.
- Write on the board a few comments they may have about the discussion.

2 Previewing the Reading

- Have the students quickly look over the photos and reading.
- Read the questions and call on students to answer them.
- Comment on the answers, if necessary.

ANSWER KEY

1. Rights of Passage—What Are Rites of Passage?; Birth Rituals in Korea; Islamic Weddings; Funerals in Thailand; The Timelessness of Rites of Passage
2. Answers will vary.
3. Questions will vary.

3 Previewing Vocabulary

- Read the directions to the students.
- Have them put a check mark (✔) next to the words they know.
- Tell them **not** to use a dictionary during this part of the lesson.
- Play the audio.

Read

4 Reading an Article

- Read the directions.
- Have students read the passage silently within a time limit (10–15 minutes) or have them follow along silently as you play the audio.
- Tell them to think about the questions they wrote for Activity 2.
- Tell them to underline any words or phrases that are new or that they don't understand. Remind them **not** to use a dictionary during this part of the lesson.
- Play the audio.

After You Read

5 Getting the Main Ideas

Best Practice

Organizing Information
Activities such as this will teach students to organize ideas chronologically into steps in a process. This will help them to recognize these steps when reading and set them out in an organized way when writing.

- Read the directions and look at the example of the first answer in the chart.
- Have students work on the activity individually.
- Call on different students to read the statements and give the answers.
- Discuss further, if necessary.

ANSWER KEY

Answers may vary.

Rite of Passage	Previous Status	Transition	New Status
vision quest	a boy	4 days isolated in a cave, not a boy or a man	a man with an adult name
birth rituals	pregnant women don't eat certain foods; doors are left open	the baby is born	mother drinks seaweed soup; no cold water for 21 days; 100-day ceremony to become member of community
Islamic wedding	two separate families	ask for hand, marriage contract, henna party, sword dance, trousseau, guests with gifts	married couple; bride comfortable in new home
Buddhist funeral	dying person listening to scriptures	death, chanting, body washed, put in coffin, cremation, music and company for comfort	spirit cut off from world and person is reborn in a new body

6 Checking Vocabulary

- Read the directions.
- Put students in pairs and remind them **not** to use a dictionary until they have completed this part of the lesson.
- Discuss the answers when students finish.

7 Making Inferences

- Read the directions.
- Put students in pairs and remind them **not** to use a dictionary until they have completed this part of the lesson.
- Discuss the answers when students finish.

ANSWER KEY

1. _✓_ In a vision quest, a boy finds out about his future career from his vision.

At the end, when he comes out of the cave, he is a man, with an adult name, and he knows what his livelihood will be.

2. _✓_ Korean parents might put a soccer ball in front of their one-year-old if they want him or her to be a great soccer player.

These days, people can add any object, such as a baseball, if they want their child to be a great baseball player.

3. ___ The Bedouin marriage contract involves money.

4. ___ People who put objects in the graves of the dead may have religious beliefs.

FOCUS

Understanding Chronology

- Direct students' attention to the words in the box.
- Ask them which words they would expect to find at the beginning, middle, and end of a paragraph.
- As the students say the words, put them on the board. Explain that *chronology* means the order in which events happen.

Beginning	**Middle**		**End**
first	after	after that	last
beginning	next	the next step	finally
second	then	at this point	

8 Understanding Chronology

- Read the directions.
- Tell students to do the activity in pairs.
- Check the answers when students finish.

ANSWER KEY

1. 3 **2.** 5 **3.** 1 **4.** 4 **5.** 2

FOCUS

Understanding Symbols

- Direct students' attention to the box.
- Write the word *SYMBOL* on the board.
- If there are any symbols in the classroom (baseball caps with logos, an item with the name of a school, city, or sports team) point them out and ask students what each one represents.
- Read the explanation.
- Say the words and have students repeat them after you.

9 Understanding Symbols

- Read the directions.
- You may want to have students do the activity in pairs.

ANSWER KEY

1. *The belief is that the smoke from the pipe goes up to the spirit world and allows power to come down.*
2. *Family members leave doors open, and do not repair rooms, doors, or fireplaces in the kitchen. All these symbolize an easy delivery.*
3. *The henna is more than just skin paint. It is associated with health, beauty, and luck.*

10 Checking Your Understanding

- Read the directions.
- Tell students to do the activity in pairs.
- Call on different students to read their questions and answers.
- Discuss further if necessary.

ANSWER KEY

Answers will vary.

11 Applying the Reading

- Read the directions.
- Put the example from page 133 on the board.
- Explain it to the students.

ANSWER KEY

Answers will vary. Here is an example:

The Rite of Passage: Graduation

Previous Status		**Transition**		**New Status**
college student	→	graduation	→	adult who can work and support himself or herself

Steps (Details)

complete coursework

take and pass exams

apply for graduation

rent cap and gown

invite family and friends

go to graduation ceremony

receive diploma

celebrate with family and friends

Symbols are the *cap and gown*, which represent the medieval dress of an academy, and the *diploma*, which represents the degree that the university awards the student.

Expansion Activity

- If students are from different countries, have those from the same country or region work together on a rite of passage.
- If students are from the same country, have them choose different rites of passage and work together in groups on the same one.
- If there is time, have them do research on the Internet and make a poster or PowerPoint presentation about the rite of passage.
- Tell them to share their findings with the class.

New Days, New Ways: Changing Rites of Passage

Before You Read

1 Identifying the Main Idea and Writing a Summary

Best Practice

Making Use of Academic Content
Activities such as this will help expand students' ability to locate main ideas in an academic text. With practice, they will learn to find them and summarize information in a paragraph quickly and accurately.

- Read the directions.
- Remind students **not** to use a dictionary during this part of the lesson.
- Check the answers when students finish.

ANSWER KEY

Answers may vary.

A. Main Idea: *Anyone can now experience a Native American vision quest, for a fee.*

Summary: *Although some Native Americans do not approve, several companies and organizations are offering non-Indians the opportunity (for a fee) to experience a vision quest that is similar to the traditional one.*

B. Main Idea: *Instead of going into debt to get married, Emirati grooms can now have group weddings.*

Summary: *The government of the United Arab Emirates (UAE) started a marriage fund to help young men stay out of debt when they get married. If they marry women from the UAE, they can have a lavish feast with entertainment.*

C. Main Idea: *These days, many Japanese couples get married in Western-style Christian weddings.*

Summary: *Instead of the traditional ceremonies of the past, many Japanese couples dress in Western clothes (tuxedo and long, white dress). They get married in a church using Christian scriptures and hymns, and exchange vows and kiss.*

D. Main Idea: *Couples in Western countries are also looking for a different wedding experience.*

Summary: *Besides unusual places, they are considering traditional weddings in other cultures, as in Goa, India, where they can be married in a typical Hindu ceremony.*

E. Main Idea: *People are also turning to unusual funerals.*

Summary: *In countries like Malaysia, musical groups sing in different languages and play a variety of music at different kinds of funerals. In other countries, they send their ashes into space, or preserve a dead body doing a favorite activity.*

Strategy

Identifying Opinions

- Write these words on the board:

FACT	information proven to be true
OPINION	ideas that people may disagree about

- Read the directions for the first part and tell the class to repeat the words after you.

Examples

bad (-ly)	favorite	interesting
beautiful	fun	surprising
brilliant	good (well)	too
exquisite	horrible	wonderful (-ly)

2 Distinguishing Facts from Opinions

- Read the directions.
- Tell the students to work as quickly as possible.
- Check the answers when students finish.

ANSWER KEY

1. fact **2.** opinion **3.** fact **4.** opinion
5. opinion **6.** fact **7.** fact **8.** opinion
9. fact **10.** opinion

3 Discussing the Reading: Conducting a Survey

Best Practice

Cultivating Critical Thinking
Activities such as this allow students to engage in critical thinking as they survey other students about a rite of passage in their culture. By conducting a survey, they will arrive at conclusions about their peers' opinions regarding traditional and non-traditional wedding ceremonies.

- Read the directions.
- Tell students to fill in the chart.
- You may want to have students use the Black Line Master for **Expansion Activity 26**.

REPRODUCIBLE

Expansion Activity

- The aim of this activity is to have students take a survey of their classmates on the topic of weddings.
- Photocopy and distribute **Black Line Master 26** "What Kind of Wedding… ?" on page BLM26 of this Teacher's Manual.
- Have students interview their classmates, or let them leave the classroom and interview other students.
- Give them 20–30 minutes to complete the survey.
- If students have access to a computer lab, have them make a bar graph comparing the data (traditional vs. non-traditional and males vs. females).
- When they finish, have them share their findings with the class.

Responding in Writing

FOCUS

Summarizing a Whole Reading

- Call on different students to read the directions.
- Write these points on the board:

—Change sentence structure:

active → passive

passive → active

—Use synonyms

—Keep technical terms

4 Discussing the Reading

- Have students choose one of the two readings they have read in this chapter to summarize.
- Have them write a one-paragraph summary alone and then compare it to that of another student.
- When they have compared their summaries, collect and check them.

5 Writing Your Own Ideas

Best Practice

Activating Prior Knowledge
Activities such as applying a concept from a reading to their personal experience will help students understand it better. Writing a letter to the teacher will enable them to explore a topic and perhaps come to a better understanding of it.

- Read the directions.
- Have students choose one of the topics listed and write you a letter for homework.
- The next day, collect the letters. Pass them around to different students in the class to read.
- Tell students to read them and write the main idea of each letter at the bottom.
- Then have students write a response to the letter on the back of the paper, telling their opinion on the topic. When students finish, have them give the letters back to the person who wrote them.
- After they have read them, collect and check them.

1 Determining Categories

Best Practice

Scaffolding Instruction
Activities such as this will allow students to remember vocabulary better by scaffolding instruction. The words they have just learned from the reading can be categorized into semantic groups and used as a scaffold upon which they can integrate new vocabulary.

- Read the directions.
- Ask students to do the activity quickly.
- Check the answers with the class.

ANSWER KEY

1. praying, chanting
2. priests, monks
3. coffin, cremation, deceased
4. organization, tribe, community, society
5. hug, cry, shout
6. proposal, wedding, coming-of-age

FOCUS

Analyzing Word Roots and Prefixes

- Read the directions.
- Read the **Prefixes** and **Word Roots** and ask students to read the **Meanings**.

2 Analyzing Word Roots and Prefixes

- Read the directions.
- Have students do the activity quickly.
- Check the answers.

ANSWER KEY

1. E **2.** C **3.** A **4.** C **5.** C **6.** E
7. A **8.** E

3 Focusing on Words from the Academic Word List

- Read the directions.
- Have students do the activity quickly.
- Check the answers.

ANSWER KEY

1. transition **2.** status **3.** incorporation
4. previous **5.** vision **6.** physically
7. community

4 Searching the Internet

Best Practice

Interacting with Others
Activities such as this will encourage students to explore a topic of interest with their peers. They will develop the skills of working together to find information and organizing it in a logical way to present it to the class.

- Read the directions.
- Have students look at the choices.
- Ask them to choose one and find a partner who chose the same one.
- You may want to have students use the Black Line Master for **Expansion Activity 27** to guide their research.

REPRODUCIBLE

Expansion Activity

- The purpose of this activity is to encourage students to do research on a topic presented in the readings.
- Photocopy and distribute **Black Line Master 27** "Rites of Passage Redone" on page BLM27 of this Teacher's Manual.
- Allow students to choose a topic and search the Internet with others who have chosen the same one.
- Have them download a photo or prepare an outline on the board to present their topic to the class.
- Remind students that each one in the group must speak during the presentation.
- Have the other students write down one or two questions to ask the group after their presentation.

FOCUS TOEFL® iBT

Topic-Sentence Patterns on the TOEFL® Internet-Based Test (iBT)

- Write these sentences from the first three paragraphs on the board:

  [A] Rites of passage are not found only in indigenous cultures. They are universal, occurring in all cultures, and include certain birthdays, coming-of-age rituals, weddings, and funerals.

  [B] Anthropologists use the term *rite of passage* for a ceremony or ritual of transition that marks a person's change from one status or social position to another.

  [C] Many cultures have a rite of passage that marks the birth of a baby. In Korean tradition, the rite begins during the woman's pregnancy.

- Read the directions.
- Call on different students to read the paragraphs.

1 Practice

- Read the directions.
- Tell students to read the passage quickly. Write a beginning and ending time on the board (10–15 minutes).
- When time is up, tell them to stop reading.

2 Identifying the Main Idea

- Go over the directions.
- Have students work individually to write their answers, then compare with other students.

ANSWER KEY

Answers may vary.

1. [A] Every society has rites of passage that fit its culture.
2. [B] Learning to drive in the United States reflects values of American culture and can be compared to other rites of passage in other cultures.
3. [C] The timing of learning to drive has great significance for the majority of Americans.
4. [D] Both family and school prepare teenagers for the transition toward adulthood, specifically learning how to drive.
5. [E] American society treasures state-issued permits and reveres the processes for obtaining them.
6. [F] America's cultural preoccupation with money is also addressed in the ritual of getting a driver's license.
7. [G] Being a driver brings deep-seated American values into play.
8. [H] Driving represents a passage from childhood into adulthood.

Self-Assessment Log

- Read the directions aloud and have students check vocabulary they learned in the chapter and are prepared to use.
- Have students check the strategies practiced in the chapter (or the degree to which they learned them). They have actually used all these strategies in Chapter 10.
- Put students in small groups. Ask students to find the information or an activity related to each strategy in the group.
- Tell students to find definitions in the chapter for any words they did not check.

REPRODUCIBLE

Expansion Activity

- The aim of this activity is to have students practice the parts of speech of words in the **Target Vocabulary** and **Vocabulary List** in **PART 1.**
- Photocopy and distribute **Black Line Master 28** "Parts of Speech" on page BLM28 of this Teacher's Manual.
- Read the directions.
- Tell students to work individually and then in pairs.
- Have students check their work using a dictionary.

Name ______________________ Date ____________ REPRODUCIBLE BLM 1

Chapter 1 Part 1: Can You Tell Me About Your Schooling?

DIRECTIONS: Take this paper and a pencil and interview a classmate. Ask your classmate the questions below. When you finish, introduce your partner to the class.

1. Where did you go to school? In what area (city/town and country)? Was it a public or a private school?

School	Public/Private	Public/Private
a. elementary school		
b. middle school		
c. high school		

2. Were the schools mixed or only for boys or girls?

3. Did you have to wear a uniform? If so, what did it look like? If not, what kind of clothing did you wear to school?

4. How did you get to and from school every day?

5. What kind of teachers did you have? (strict / kind / boring / interesting / old / young / etc.)?

6. Who was your favorite teacher? Why?

7. What subjects were you good in / not so good in?

8. What other activities did you participate in at school, such as sports or clubs?

Name ______________________ Date ______________ REPRODUCIBLE BLM 2

Chapter 1 Part 2: Can You Tell Me Your Opinion?

DIRECTIONS: Take this paper and a pencil and interview five people. Ask them their opinion about the positive and negative aspects of the educational system in their country. Take notes on their answers. When you finish, report your findings to the class.

Name/Country	Positive Aspects of Educational System	Negative Aspects of Educational System
1. Name: Country:		
2. Name: Country:		
3. Name: Country:		
4. Name: Country:		
5. Name: Country:		

Name ______________________ Date ______________ REPRODUCIBLE BLM 3

Chapter 1 Part 3: Find a College or University That...

DIRECTIONS: Use the Internet to look up the following information. Be sure to write down the name of the college/university, its location, and its web address (URL) so that other students can find it. For item 7, you can choose a university that has features you find interesting. When you finish, share your research with other students.

Find a college or university that...

1. is near a river: *Boston University* *Boston, MA (USA)* *www.bu.edu*
2. offers scholarships to foreign students: ______________________
3. offers classes in horseback riding: ______________________
4. allows students to spend one year studying abroad: ______________________
5. offers classes in Chinese, Japanese, and Korean: ______________________
6. has a Medical School: ______________________
7. ______________________ (your choice): ______________________

Share your answers with other students and copy their answers here:

Name ______________________ Date ______________ REPRODUCIBLE **BLM 4**

Chapter 2 Part 1: Major Cities

DIRECTIONS: Choose a country. Draw a simple map of that country. Write the names of three major cities.

Country ______________________

Cities ______________________

Look up your country online and write the following information below about one of the cities. Present your findings to the class.

1. Population: ______________________
2. Problems in the city: ______________________
3. Mass transit system: ______________________
4. Recycling program: ______________________
5. Homeless people/programs: ______________________
6. Environmental programs: ______________________

Name ______________________ Date ______________ REPRODUCIBLE BLM 5

Chapter 2 Part 2: City Life In The Future

DIRECTIONS: Take this paper and a pencil and interview at least three people. Ask them their opinion about city life in the future. Take notes on their answers. When you finish, report your findings to the class.

1. Name	
Will city life be better or worse than it is today?	Why? 1. 2.
How will city life be different from what it is today?	Predictions: 1. 2. 3.
2. Name	
Will city life be better or worse than it is today?	Why? 1. 3.
How will city life be different from what it is today?	Predictions: 1. 2. 3.
3. Name	
Will city life be better or worse than it is today?	Why? 1. 2.
How will city life be different from what it is today?	Predictions: 1. 2. 3.

Name ______________________________ Date ______________ REPRODUCIBLE BLM 6

Chapter 2 Part 3: English-Language Newspapers

DIRECTIONS: Take this paper and a pencil and go to the computer lab or use your own computer. With a partner, use a search engine (like Google) to find the name of an English-language newspaper in the country assigned by your instructor. Read an article about the capital city of that country and write about the main ideas and details. When you finish, report your findings to the class.

Country: ______________________________

Name of newspaper: ______________________________

Main Ideas	**Details**
1.	**1.**
	2.
	3.
2.	**1.**
	2.
	3.
3.	**1.**
	2.
	3.
4.	**1.**
	2.
	3.

Name ______________________ Date ____________ REPRODUCIBLE BLM 7

Chapter 3 Part 1: Venn Diagrams

DIRECTIONS: Take this paper and pencil and choose 2 sets of persons, places, or things that have both similarities <u>and</u> differences. When you finish, share your diagrams with two other students.

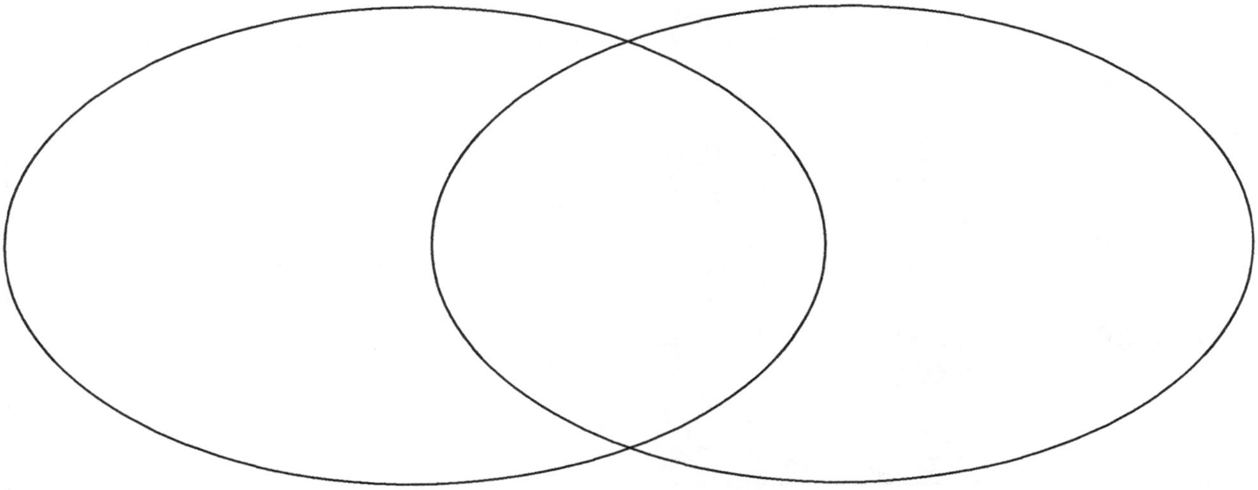

____

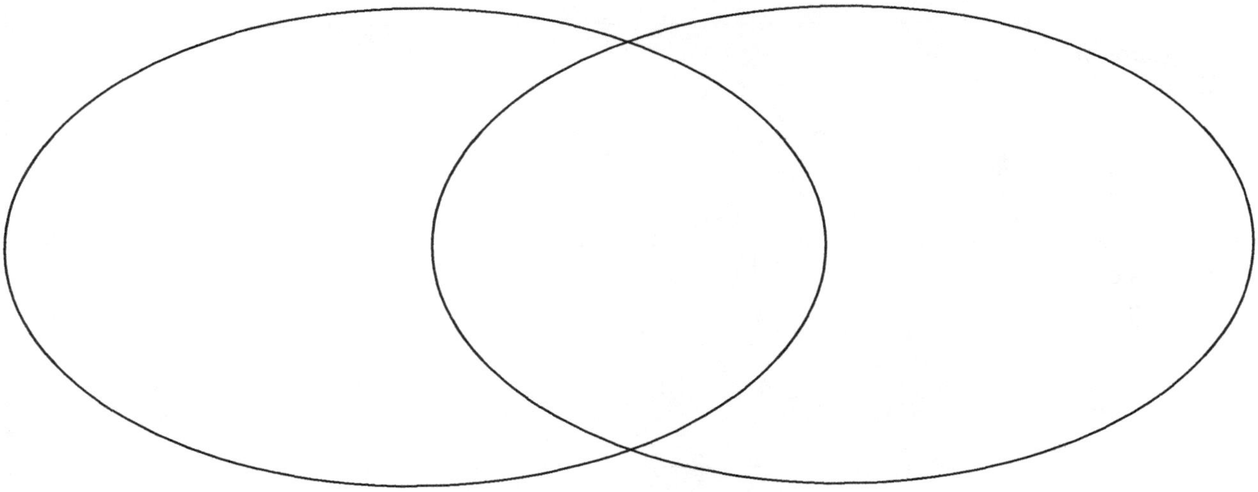

____

Name ______________________ Date ______________ REPRODUCIBLE BLM 8

Chapter 3 Part 2: Consumer Organizations In My Country

DIRECTIONS: Take this paper and with a partner look up a consumer organization in your country. Make sure it is different from those of the other students. When you finish, report your findings to the class.

Name and Logo		
History (When? Who?)		
Purpose		
Programs or Events		
Sources of Funding		
Number of Members		

Name ______________________ Date ____________ REPRODUCIBLE BLM 9

Chapter 3 Part 2: Analyzing Advertisements

A. Choose a product with your group. Each member will look in a different magazine or at a different website for an advertisement of this product and bring it to class. Write short answers to these questions about your advertisement. Share your answers with your group.

1. What is your group's product? ____________________
2. How does your advertisement show the product? ____________________
3. Are there any people in the picture? How do they look? What are they doing? ____________________
4. What do you think this product does for them? ____________________
5. How do you think they feel about this product? ____________________
6. What are some of the words or expressions used in the advertisement? ____________________

   ____
7. What do they mean? ____________________
8. How do you feel about this product? ____________________
9. Would you buy it? Why or why not? ____________________
10. What kind of psychology is used? ____________________

B. Write a short paragraph about your advertisement. Include some of the answers to the questions above. Then show your advertisement to the class and analyze it.

In this advertisement, we see…

____

____

____

____

____

____

____

____

____

____

____

____

Name ______________________ Date ______________ REPRODUCIBLE BLM 10

Chapter 4 Part 1: Cell Phone Use

DIRECTIONS: Every time you use your cell phone, put a check (✓) in one of the columns. Later you will use these data to make a pie chart to show the percentage of use for each category.

Day	Made Call	Received Call	Sent Text	Received Text	Sent Image	Received Image
Monday						
Tuesday						
Wednesday						
Thursday						
Friday						
Saturday						
Sunday						
Total						

- Put a check each time you make or receive a call, send or receive text messages or images (photos or videos).
- Show your cell phone log to your partner every day.
- At the end of the week, write the total in each column.
- Take your log to the computer lab with your partner and make pie charts of your cell phone use. If you are not sure how to do this, ask for help.
- Share your pie charts with the class.
- Give your log to the teacher. A classmate will make pie charts of the cell phone use of men and of women and the whole class.
- Put all the pie charts on a poster board or bulletin board to share with the class.

Name ______________________ Date ____________ REPRODUCIBLE BLM 11

Chapter 4 Part 2: Survey of Globalized Countries

DIRECTIONS: Take this paper and a pencil and interview 10 people in the category your group has chosen (nationality or age group). When you finish, make a bar graph and share your data displays with other groups in the class.

Questions:

1. Do you have a cell phone?
2. Do you have a computer?
3. Are you interested in the politics of your country?
4. Does your country have many international visitors?
5. Does your country have a strong economy?

Nationality or Age Group ________	Cell Phone Y/N	Computer Y/N	Politics Y/N	International Visitors Y/N	Strong Economy Y/N
1 M					
2 M					
3 M					
4 M					
5 M					
6 F					
7 F					
8 F					
9 F					
10 F					
Total					

Answers: Yes = Y; No = N

M=Male; F=Female

Chapter 4 Part 3: Online Job Boards

A. Underline the website that you and your partner chose in class (www.careerbuilder.com; jobsjobs.com; www.jobster.com; www.jobweb.com; www.monster.com) and find it on the Internet. Explore the online job board and answer the following questions.

Useful job-related information:

1. ______________________________
2. ______________________________
3. ______________________________
4. ______________________________
5. ______________________________

B. Rate this online job site by circling a number for each category.

	worst		satisfactory		best
Attractive site	1	2	3	4	5
Easy to find information	1	2	3	4	5
Many jobs listed	1	2	3	4	5
Process clear	1	2	3	4	5
Easy to ask questions	1	2	3	4	5

C. If you have a résumé or curriculum vitae, apply online for one of the jobs that you are qualified for. Report to the class on the response that you get.

Name ______________________________ Date ______________ REPRODUCIBLE BLM 13

Chapter 5 Part 1: Happiness Poll

DIRECTIONS: Take this paper and a pencil and interview 5 other students. Ask them to rate the qualities that measure happiness for their country. Ask if they believe the quality to be *excellent*, *average*, or *poor* in their country and write that in the box under each quality. When you finish, share your findings with the class.

Name	Country	Income	Health and Safety	Education	Balance of Work and Leisure	Happiness
1.						
2.						
3.						
4.						
5.						

Compare your answers with your classmates to see if there are any similarities or differences in opinion.

____

____

____

____

____

____

Chapter 6 Part 1: Analyzing a Country's Endangered Food

DIRECTIONS: With a partner, go to the computer lab or work independently at home. Find the website for the Ark of Taste on the Slow Food Foundation for Biodiversity: http://www.slowfoodfoundation.org. Find your country or a country you know. Fill in the information below.

1. Name of country/region of the world: ______________________
2. What are its neighboring countries? ______________________
3. How many products are endangered for the country you chose? ________
4. What are some fruits or vegetables that are endangered? ______________________

   ____
5. Are there some animal breeds that are endangered? What are they? ______________________

   ____
6. What are some other products that are endangered? ______________________

   ____
7. You can contact the Slow Food Foundation for Biodiversity by e-mail. What is their e-mail address? ______________________
8. In what country are the official headquarters for the Slow Food Foundation for Biodiversity located? ______________________

Name ______________________ Date ____________ REPRODUCIBLE **BLM 15**

Chapter 6 Part 2: Reality TV Shows

DIRECTIONS: Take this paper and a pencil and go to the computer lab with a partner or do the assignment at home. Look up a reality show on the Internet in the country you have chosen. Write the answers to the questions. When you finish, give a short report to the class.

1. Name of Reality TV Show: ______________________
2. Country: ______________________
3. Summary: ______________________
4. Participants/Winner: ______________________
5. Opinion of the show: ______________________
6. Ask another student if they would like to watch this show. Ask them why or why not.

Name ______________________ Date ______________ REPRODUCIBLE **BLM 16**

Chapter 6 Part 4: Matching Idioms

DIRECTIONS: Take this paper and a pencil and copy the idioms from the board after the team activity. Use it as a study aid to help you learn the idioms.

1. stories that are sad and make people cry ______________________
2. live in a simple, uncomfortable way ______________________
3. far away and difficult to reach ______________________
4. is eliminated, removed ______________________
5. compete with each other ______________________
6. It's obvious/It's unnecessary to say, but... ______________________
7. a lot ______________________
8. probably ______________________
9. fast ______________________
10. competed with great energy ______________________
11. become wildly popular, especially online ______________________
12. situations where people move quickly from poor to rich ______________________

Name ______________________ Date ______________ REPRODUCIBLE BLM 17

Chapter 7 Part 1: Find Someone Who...

DIRECTIONS: Take this paper and a pencil. Stand up, move around the classroom. Ask classmates the questions below. When someone answers yes, write his or her name on the line. When someone answers no, ask another question. When you finish, introduce your partner to the class.

Example **A:** Do you have a dog?
B: No, I have a bird, a canary.
A: How does it communicate with you?
B: It sings to me.
A: Great. What's your name?

Do you have... ?	How does it/do they communicate with you?
1. a dog? Name ______	
2. cat? Name ______	
3. a bird? Name ______	
4. a fish or turtle? Name ______	
5. a mouse, rat, hamster, or gerbil? Name ______	
6. a horse, donkey, or camel? Name ______	
7. more than one pet? Name ______	
8. animals outside your house? Name ______	
9. animals that you ride? Name ______	

Name ______________________ Date ______________

REPRODUCIBLE **BLM 18**

Chapter 7 Part 2: Toys for Girls and Boys

DIRECTIONS: Take this paper and a pencil and look at two different websites with your group. In the first column, make a list of three toys advertised for girls, three for boys, and three for both. In the second column, put *SI* for *social-interactive* and *TO* for *task-oriented.* In the third column, write a short description of how children might play with the toys. Be prepared to present your list to the class.

Toys for Girls	SI/TO	Description of Game/Activity
1. *My Little Pony*	*SI*	*Each girl takes a pony to one girl's house to have a "pony party." Each girl "talks" for her pony as it plays with the other ponies. Game ends when party ends.*
2.		
3.		
Toys for Boys	**SI/TO**	**Description of Game/Activity**
1. *Action Figures*	*TO*	*Each boy takes an action figure outside to play with. They all fight together against a common enemy. Game ends when enemy is overcome.*
2.		
3.		
Toys for Both	**SI/TO**	**Description of Game/Activity**
1.		
2.		
3.		

Name ______________________ Date ____________ REPRODUCIBLE BLM 19

Chapter 7 Part 4: Slang Expressions

DIRECTIONS: Take this paper and a pencil and look at the slang expressions in Part I. Try to guess the meaning of each one and write it in Standard American English (SAE). Your instructor will help you. Then think of words or phrases in your language that come from English in Part II. Write them the way they are spelled in your language and in English. Then write a "pure" word in your language with the same/similar meaning. Be prepared to present your list to the class.

Part I

Slang expressions	Standard American English
'S up?	
A'ight.	
Latah!	
Gotcha!	
Dunno.	

Part II

Your Language	English	"Pure" Word

Chapter 8 Part 1: Traveling the Silk Road

DIRECTIONS: With a partner choose a country or region along the Silk Road and one of the products grown or made there that was transported by the merchants in caravans. Use the Internet to locate information on your topic. When you finish, share your findings with the class.

1. Name of country or region: ______________________________

   ____

2. History of settlers or migrants: ______________________________

   ____

3. Major cities: ______________________________

   ____

4. Climate and agriculture: ______________________________

   ____

5. Natural resources and products: ______________________________

   ____

6. How product was made: ______________________________

   ____

7. Which countries bought and used the product: ______________________________

   ____

8. Present-day use of produce: ______________________________

   ____

Name ______________________ Date ______________ REPRODUCIBLE **BLM 21**

Chapter 8 Part 2: Beauty Treatments

DIRECTIONS: Take this paper and a pencil and go to the computer lab with a partner or small group. Look on a website about beauty treatments and fill in the chart below. When you have finished, present your findings to the class.

Name of treatment	
Place of treatment	
People giving it/ training	
People getting it	
Equipment needed	
Steps in treatment	
Cost per visit	
Results of treatment	
Benefits/ Dangers	

Name ______________________ Date ____________ REPRODUCIBLE BLM 22

Chapter 8 Part 4: Spelling and Synonyms

DIRECTIONS: Take this paper and a pencil and write the words that your teacher or classmates dictate to you in the first column. Then write a synonym or meaning for the word in the second column.

Spelling	Synonym/Meaning
1.	
2.	
3.	
4.	
5.	
6.	
7.	
8.	
9.	
10.	
11.	
12.	
13.	
14.	
15.	

Name ______________________ Date ______________ REPRODUCIBLE **BLM 23**

Chapter 9 Part 1: Improving Your Brain

DIRECTIONS: With a partner, choose one of the suggestions given in paragraphs H and I, or others that you can think of. Use the Internet to locate information on your topic. When you finish, share your findings with the class.

Good for your brain	Bad for your brain
Activities:	Activities:
Food/Drink:	Food/Drink:
Other:	Other:
What I'll start doing:	What I'll start doing:

Name ______________________ Date ______________ REPRODUCIBLE BLM 24

Chapter 9 Part 2: Violence and Genetics

DIRECTIONS: Take this paper and a pencil and go to the computer lab with a partner or small group. Look for an article on the Internet about the link between violence and genetics and fill in the chart below. When you have finished, present your findings to the class.

Name of article and author(s)	
Place where study was done	
Group of people studied	
Background of people	
Scientific explanation	
Other comments	
Possible treatments	
Social consequences	
Prevention of violence	
Your opinion	

Name ______________________ Date ______________ REPRODUCIBLE BLM 25

Chapter 9 Part 4: Parts of Speech

DIRECTIONS: Take this paper and a pencil and write the parts of speech in each column without using a dictionary. Some words do not have all four word forms. When you finish, check your answers with a partner, using a dictionary if necessary.

NOUN	VERB	ADJECTIVE	ADVERB
1. evidence	______	______	
2.	imply	______	______
3.	______	insightful	
4.	______		intelligently
5. maturity			
6.	memorize	______	______
7. logic	______		
8.	involve		______
9. ______	______	mental	
10.	______		traditionally

Chapter 10 Part 2: What Kind of Wedding… ?

DIRECTIONS: Take this paper and a pencil and interview the students in your class or outside your class. Record how many people answer "traditional" and "nontraditional." Take notes on the reasons for their answers.

What kind of wedding do you prefer: traditional or nontraditional?	
Traditional	**Nontraditional**
Why? What are your favorite parts?	What is your idea of a good nontraditional wedding? (What are the elements?)
# of males # of females	# of males # of females

Chapter 10 Part 3: Rites of Passage Redone

DIRECTIONS: Take this paper and a pencil and go to the computer lab with a partner or small group. Look for an article on the Internet about nontraditional rites of passage and fill in the chart below. When you have finished, present your findings to the class.

Rite of passage	
People who did it	
Place where it was done	
Way it was done	
People who attended	
How much it cost	
Other comments	
Would you like to do it?	
How would you change it?	
Other comments	

Name ______________________ Date ______________ REPRODUCIBLE **BLM 28**

Chapter 10 Part 4: Parts of Speech

DIRECTIONS: Take this paper and a pencil and write the parts of speech in each column without using a dictionary. Some words do not have all four word forms. When you finish, check your answers with a partner, using a dictionary if necessary.

NOUN	VERB	ADJECTIVE	ADVERB
1.	chant		———
2. community	———		
3.	cremate		———
4. incorporation			———
5. ———	———	indigenous	
6. negotiations			———
7.	———	physical	
8. ———	———		previously
9. rite	———		
10.			transitionally
11.	vary	———	———

2. Asthma attacks may be triggered by ______.
   (A) chemicals and smog
   (B) dogs and cats
   (C) dust and insects
   (D) all of the above
3. To control asthma, most people ______.
   (A) carry inhalers
   (B) get injections
   (C) go to the hospital
   (D) stay home
4. To avoid having asthma attacks, people can ______.
   (A) keep fish or turtles as pets
   (B) ride more trucks and buses
   (C) start smoking
   (D) stop cleaning their house
5. Asthmatics should ______.
   (A) carry several inhalers
   (B) get injections every week
   (C) protect themselves from pollutants
   (D) wait for scientists to find a cure

SECTION II Strategy Look at the highlighted words and then match Column A with Column B. *(3 points each)*

Column A	Column B
1. ______ asthmatic	a. asthma
2. ______ chronic	b. buses and trucks
3. ______ indoor pollutants	c. cats and dogs
4. ______ inhaler	d. causes a reaction
5. ______ injection	e. chemicals, dust, and smog
6. ______ long-haired pets	f. cigarette smoke, dirt, insects
7. ______ outdoor pollutants	g. contains medicine for asthmatics
8. ______ respiratory illness	h. having difficulty breathing
9. ______ triggers	i. medicine given under skin with needle
10. ______ vehicles	j. over a long period of time

SECTION III New Words New Words Fill in the blanks with words from the Academic Word List from the Chapter 2. *(3 points each)*

access	environment	established	focused	global
method	predict	residents	solve	transportation

Asthma is usually common in countries where there is a lot of pollution in the ________ (1) from industry and different types of ________ (2) such as ships and trains. However, it has become a ________ (3) problem; that is, countries with large rural areas also have high rates of asthma. A doctor in Jamaica decided to find out why asthma was increasing among young rural ________ (4) where pollution didn't seem to be a problem. She noticed that more children had asthma attacks when it was windy. She asked a scientist who was studying weather patterns to find out if there was a connection. The scientist, also a woman, developed a ________ (5) of collecting what was blowing in the wind. Together they ________ (6) a connection between the amount of dust in the wind and the number of asthmas attacks on the island. The scientist also discovered that some of the dust had actually blown to Jamaica from the dry regions of Africa across the Atlantic Ocean. With a way to ________ (7) when asthma attacks were going to occur, the doctor ________ (8) on giving the rural population ________ (9) to weather forecasts so that asthmatics would stay indoors on windy days. A public health campaign helped to ________ (10) the problem and lower the number of asthma attacks.

Name ______________________ Date ______________ Score ______________

CHAPTER 2 Test Interactions 2 Reading

Asthma

SECTION I Reading Comprehension Answer these questions about the reading passage. *(3 points each)*

A Respiratory illnesses such as asthma have increased greatly in the past few decades. It is estimated that 5% of the population in the United States has asthma, which is a chronic disease, that is, it affects a person over a long period of time. It may begin before a child is 10 years old, or it may begin in adulthood. Childhood asthma usually disappears around the age of 20, but adults who get it later may have it all their lives.

B People who suffer from asthma have difficulty breathing because the airways in their lungs contract when a trigger causes a reaction. Among the triggers of asthma are indoor and outdoor pollutants, according to doctors. Since pollution has become more common, the number of people affected by this disorder has risen. Indoor pollutants include cigarette smoke, dirt, insects, and even pets like dogs or cats. Outdoor pollutants include chemicals, dust, and smog, that is, smoke from factories or transport vehicles like buses and trucks.

C People with asthma usually carry an inhaler in case of an attack. This inhaler contains medicine that they breathe in, making the contracted airways in the lungs expand so that they can breathe normally again. For a few people with severe asthma, medicine can also be given by injection—in other words, it can be applied under the skin with a needle every few weeks to prevent attacks.

D While it is not possible to cure this condition, people who suffer from it are advised to avoid pollutants. Parents with asthmatic children are told not to smoke in the house and not to keep long-haired pets. They need to clean the house frequently and keep it free of insects. Asthmatic adults are told to avoid outdoor areas with a lot of pollution and working environments with a lot of chemicals.

E Scientists continue to search for a cure for asthma, but instead of waiting for one, people with asthma can take an active role in protecting themselves. By avoiding asthma triggers, carrying an inhaler, living in a clean, smoke-free house, and working in a pollutant-free place, they can live healthier lives.

1. Childhood asthma usually ________.
   (A) appears when children are 5
   (B) appears before children are 10
   (C) disappears after children are 10
   (D) disappears before children are 20

SECTION IV Building Vocabulary Use the words in the box to complete the sentences below. A word can be used more than once. *(3 points each)*

about	in	one	to
for	into	other	up

1. In our English class, the teacher often separates us ______________ groups.
2. She separates us according ______________ our ability.
3. This is ______________ contrast ______________ our history class, where we never work in groups.
4. On the ______________ hand, some smart students do not worry ______________ their tests because they always get good grades.
5. On the ______________ hand, even smart students should study.
6. The road ______________ success can sometimes be challenging.
7. ______________ this reason, it's important to never give ______________. You must keep studying and trying.

TOTAL _____/100 pts.

SECTION IV Building Vocabulary Write the missing noun, verb, adjective or adverb in the numbered boxes. *(2 points each)*

Noun	Verb	Adjective	Adverb
difference	1. ______	different	2. ______
3. ______	pollute	4. ______	
prediction	5. ______	predictable	6. ______
7. ______	save	8. ______	safely
9. ______	solve	10. ______	

Complete the sentences below with words from the preceding chart. Use one word from each row of the chart. *(1 point each)*

11. Countries around the world have ______ rates of asthma, depending on the amount of pollution.
12. Asthma attacks in Jamaica are ______ because they usually occur when it's windy.
13. The ______ to the problem was to warn asthmatics to stay indoors on windy days.
14. When factories ______ a lake or river, the fish often die.
15. This means that people cannot ______ swim in water that is polluted.

TOTAL ____/100 pts.

Name ______________________ Date ______________ Score ______________

CHAPTER 3 Test Interactions 2 Reading

The Consumers Union

SECTION I Reading Comprehension Answer these questions about the reading passage. *(3 points each)*

A The Consumers Union (CU) was founded in 1936 to give information and advice to the public about goods and services. By doing research in laboratories and conducting tests on products, scientists were able to rate them, or tell if they were good or bad. They started by testing food like milk and cereal—and then personal products like soap and stockings. There were three categories in their ratings: *Best Buy*, *Also Acceptable*, and *Not Acceptable*. Later, CU began testing cars and home appliances, such as fans, radios, and other small machines.

B In the same year it was founded, the organization began publishing a magazine for its members, *Consumers Union Reports*, listing the ratings of products that they tested. In 1940, CU sent out a questionnaire, that is, a list of questions, to its members, asking them to rate the products that they used. This questionnaire became so popular that it has continued until today. In 1942, the magazine's name was changed to *Consumer Reports* and sold to the general public.

C By the 1950s, the number of people buying *Consumer Reports* (CR) reached 400,000. During this decade, the magazine reported on the dangers of tobacco, the poor quality of color TV sets, the contamination of milk by nuclear testing, and other news that was controversial, or caused debate. In the 1960s, the magazine reported that the price of auto insurance varied widely, or was different, among companies. In the 1970s, it reported on the pollution of America's drinking water by factories. These articles won national prizes because they informed the public about problems that needed to be solved.

D In the 1980s, *CR* began publishing special newsletters for different readers on cars, travel, health, and even one for children on how to earn and save money. In the 1990s, the Consumers Union moved to a new testing and research center with 50 modern laboratories in Yonkers, New York. By this time, *CR* had over 5 million magazine readers and 1 million online readers. After 80 years, this organization is still protecting consumers from the false claims of advertisers and the dangers of unsafe products.

1. The Consumers Union started to publish a magazine ______.
   - (A) in 1936
   - (B) in 1940
   - (C) in the 1980s
   - (D) in the 1990s

2. The magazine was sold only to members until ______.
   (A) 1936
   (B) 1940
   (C) 1942
   (D) 1960
3. In the 1950s, *CR* didn't report on ______.
   (A) bad TV sets
   (B) contaminated milk
   (C) tobacco's dangers
   (D) polluted drinking water
4. The magazine won prizes because ______.
   (A) it rated products
   (B) it told the public about problems
   (C) some products were not acceptable
   (D) there were so many problems
5. After 70 years, people ______.
   (A) are still reading *CR*
   (B) are tired of reading *CR*
   (C) believe the false claims of advertisers
   (D) buy unsafe products

SECTION II Strategy Look back at the highlighted words and then do the activity below. *(3 points each)*

1. To rate means ______.
   (A) to conduct tests on products
   (B) to do research in laboratories
   (C) to tell if products are good or bad
   (D) to test food and personal products
2. Home appliances are ______.
   (A) cars
   (B) milk and cereal
   (C) small machines
   (D) soap and stockings
3. A questionnaire is ______.
   (A) a list of questions
   (B) a magazine
   (C) ratings of products
   (D) so popular

4. The word controversial in paragraph B probably means ______.
   (A) causing debate
   (B) contamination
   (C) dangerous
   (D) other news

5. The word varied in paragraph C is closest in meaning to ______.
   (A) very cheap
   (B) very expensive
   (C) was changing
   (D) was different

SECTION III New Words Fill in the blanks with words from the Academic Word List from Chapter 3. *(3 points each)*

capacity	common knowledge	consumes	economy	funds
grants	influenced	item	sport utility vehicle	success

After reading about the Consumers Union (CU), you may wonder how scientists test the products. It is ______(1) that CU buys all the products that it tests. If a company sends an ______(2), CU returns it because it does not want to be ______(3) by the company. The ______(4) of its testing is based on the independence of its testing. CU is supported by ______(5) collected from members and ______(6) from other sources. It does not accept any money from companies. To rate a car like a ______(7), a driver takes it to the auto-test facility in Connecticut. There he will find out the ______(8) of the car, or how many people and how much equipment will fit inside. Next, he will drive it around for several hours to see what its fuel ______(9) is, or how much gas it ______(10). Then, he will drive it in rainy and snowy weather and in rocky and hilly areas to see how fast it goes and how safely it stops. Finally, he and a team of other drivers will look at the data and give the SUV a rating.

SECTION IV Building Vocabulary Are the following words nouns or adjectives? On the lines write n. for noun or adj. for adjective. *(2 points each)*

______ **1.** information	______ **6.** dissatisfaction
______ **2.** identical	______ **7.** marketers
______ **3.** social	______ **8.** violent
______ **4.** subsidiary	______ **9.** influential
______ **5.** offensive	______ **10.** advantage

Complete the sentences below with words from the preceding exercise. Use a different word for each sentence. *(2 points each)*

11. ______________ try to influence consumers to buy products.

12. Some advertisements ______________ are because they are not true.

13. People often show their ______________ with a product by returning it.

14. Before you buy a product, get as much ______________ about it as possible.

15. You will have an ______________ if you compare products before you buy them.

16. If you buy two ______________ products, one may not work as well as the other.

17. In a ______________ snowstorm, it is dangerous to drive, even in an SUV.

18. A company may have a ______________ in another country.

19. If CU allows companies to send them free products, this may be ______________ on how CU rates the product.

20. CU performs ______________ a service when it tells the public about unsafe products.

TOTAL ____/100 pts.

Name ______________________ Date ______________ Score ______________

CHAPTER 4 Test — Interactions 2 Reading

Career Change

SECTION I Reading Comprehension Answer these questions about the reading passage. *(3 points each)*

A People who are thinking about changing careers are often afraid of what will happen if they quit their job. Will they find another one? Will they like another field as well as the one they are in now? Will they be able to grow and advance in a new organization?

B As these questions come to mind, they should try to figure out the answers so they can reach a decision. Although there is a high rate of unemployment in some countries, there are usually jobs for skilled workers who can use computers or other equipment. Those who have specialized training in these areas can generally find a position without too much effort.

C The question of whether they'll like another field more than their current one is also a crucial one. While it's nice to dream about having another job, the reality may be that they aren't suited for it. For example, if an architect likes to cook but has no idea about how to run a business, it may be risky for him to open a restaurant. He can cook for his friends on weekends and satisfy his dreams of being a chef in that way.

D Another good way for a person to find out if she will be successful in a new field is to try it out as a part-time job. Being an event planner sounds glamorous, but helping friends with parties or weddings might show her that it's also very stressful. However, if she has the creativity and organization necessary for such a position, she can continue to plan events for friends until she builds up a reputation. Then she can leave her current job to look for a job in event planning knowing that she'll be successful in this area.

E Once a person has found his or her specialty and decides on the change, it's necessary to stick with it until the business gets off the ground. This usually takes about five years. If the move has been from one company to another, the person should stay until it is clear he is doing a good job and can advance to a higher position. Following this advice will make the transition smoother and the career change successful.

1. According to the reading, people who think about changing careers generally ______.
   - (A) quit their jobs
   - (B) are afraid of quitting their jobs
   - (C) find another one right away
   - (D) grow and advance in a new organization

2. There is a high rate of unemployment in some countries, but skilled workers _______.
   (A) lose their jobs
   (B) try to reach a decision
   (C) use computers
   (D) with training can still get jobs
3. If a person dreams about doing another job, _______.
   (A) he is suited for it
   (B) he can run a business
   (C) he still may not be able to do it
   (D) he will be satisfied as a chef
4. Having a part-time job _______.
   (A) is a good way to try another career
   (B) sounds glamorous
   (C) is very stressful
   (D) builds up a person's career
5. You should stay in a new career at least five years because _______.
   (A) it's your specialty
   (B) you moved from one company to another
   (C) you can do a good job and advance in that time
   (D) the transition will be smoother

SECTION II Strategy Look back at the highlighted words and then do the activity below. *(3 points each)*

1. An event planner is a person who _______.
   (A) helps friends
   (B) sounds glamorous
   (C) is very stressful
   (D) arranges parties and weddings
2. To stick with it means to _______.
   (A) find a specialty
   (B) decide on a change
   (C) stay for a few years
   (D) change companies
3. A business that gets off the ground _______.
   (A) is successful
   (B) stays until it is clear
   (C) can advance to a higher position
   (D) makes a smooth transition

4. The pronoun those in paragraph B refers to ______.
- (A) jobs
- (B) skilled workers
- (C) computers
- (D) areas

5. The pronoun it in paragraph D refers to ______.
- (A) another good way
- (B) a new field
- (C) creativity
- (D) organization

SECTION III New Words Fill in the blanks with words from the Academic Word List from Chapter 4. *(4 points each)*

career counselors	job security	keep up with	leisure	telecommuting
on the move	outsourcing	overworked	stress	upgrade

Nowadays, workers are ______(1), changing careers for many reasons. Some have lost their jobs due to ______(2) caused by companies searching for cheaper labor. Others feel that they are ______(3), and are looking for a job with less ______(4). Still others need to take time off to ______(5) their skills and learn more about computers so they can ______(6) the latest technology. Some ______(7) advise people looking for work to consider several things before they accept another position. First of all, if they just lost a job, they should ask about the ______(8) of the next one. Second, they should make sure they have enough ______(9) time so they don't feel so pressured by the demands of work. Third, they should consider ______(10), if possible, and working from a home office. This way, they'll have time to take courses that build their skills so they can get a better job in the future.

SECTION IV Building Vocabulary Find the words in the box that complete the following phrases and write them in the blanks. Each word can only be used one time. *(3 points each)*

agencies	classified	confidence	drawbacks	hopping
manufacturing	part	personnel	workforce	worldwide

1. A great number of ________________ jobs have been outsourced to Asia, and factories here have closed.
2. To find a job quickly, go to ________________ the ads of an online job board.
3. Some people enjoy job ________________, while others prefer to stay at one company for many years.
4. To work in sales, a person needs a lot of self-________________.
5. Although mothers sometimes take ________________-time jobs to stay home with young children, most women need to work full-time.
6. Everybody has a dream job in mind, but the reality is that all types of work have ________________.
7. Employment ________________ usually charge the company looking for workers a fee, not the people looking for jobs.
8. Now there are more women in the ________________ than ever before.
9. Many universities have a ________________ office where students can find work after graduation.
10. The decrease in manufacturing jobs is about eleven percent ________________.

TOTAL _____/100 pts.

Name ______________________ Date ______________ Score ______________

An Ancient Art

SECTION I Reading Comprehension Answer these questions about the reading passage. *(3 points each)*

A Although tattoos seem like a recent fad in the United States, they actually have a long history as a form of body decoration. In some cultures, they were considered beautiful works of art. Ancient tribes in Japan and China, clans in northern Europe, and religious groups around the Mediterranean all wore tattoos. The word probably comes from "tatu," meaning "to mark" in Tahitian, the language of an island in the South Pacific.

B In the 1700s, when Captain James Cook sailed from England to the South Pacific, many of his sailors got tattoos. They went back to Europe and showed them to others, and this practice became common among seamen. They enthusiastically accepted the painful experience to bring artwork back home on their bodies. From sailors, this custom gradually spread to the upper class in Europe, and in the1800s, it was a custom for rich gentlemen to travel to the Pacific islands and Asia to get tattooed by famous artists. In fact, many of the males in the royal families of Europe—princes and kings—had tattoos.

C At that time, tattooing was still done by hand, that is, artists made tiny holes in the skin with a needle or other sharp object. Then they put ink of different colors into the holes, according to a design. Nowadays, artists use electric tattoo machines, which make hundreds of holes at once, automatically pushing the ink into the skin. What used to be a long painful process takes much less time, although it still hurts! After a few days, depending on the size of the tattoo, the skin heals, or gets better, and the tattoo can be distinguished.

D In the past decade, many young people in the United States have started getting tattoos, bringing this ancient art form to life again. A third of Americans in their 20s have tattoos, while a fourth of those in their 30s have them. Tattoos are more common in Western countries, where about 20% of the population has at least one tattoo. Is this a trend or just a fad? If we look at history, we can probably call it a long-term fad. In the 19th century, tattoos were fashionable for a few decades, and who knows? They may continue to be popular for many years to come.

1. Tattoos were popular among _______.
   (A) ancient tribes
   (B) island cultures
   (C) European royalty
   (D) all of the above

2. Captain Cook's sailors got tattooed in ______.
   - (A) Asia
   - (B) England
   - (C) the Pacific islands
   - (D) Europe

3. Gentlemen, princes, and kings were tattooed by ______.
   - (A) artists doing work by hand
   - (B) Captain Cook
   - (C) electric tattoo machines
   - (D) sailors

4. Nowadays, getting a tattoo ______ than before.
   - (A) hurts more
   - (B) is faster
   - (C) is less painful
   - (D) is more distinguished

5. In the United States, ______ have tattoos.
   - (A) 25% of people in their 20s
   - (B) 20% of people in their 30s
   - (C) more than half of people in their 20s and 30s
   - (D) a third of all people

SECTION II Strategy Look back at the reading and match Column A with Column B. *(3 points each)*

Column A	Column B
1. ______ heals	a. fashionable
2. ______ needle	b. form of art
3. ______ is painful	c. rich gentlemen
4. ______ popular	d. gets better
5. ______ royal family males	e. hurts
6. ______ sailors	f. language of a South Pacific Island
7. ______ Tahitian	g. princes and kings
8. ______ tattoo	h. sail
9. ______ travel	i. seamen
10. ______ upper class	j. sharp object

SECTION III New Words Complete the paragraph with words from the Academic Word List from Chapter 5. *(3 points each)*

areas	components	economic	income	researchers
complex	concept	environment	psychological	trend

The art of tattooing came to the western world in the 1700s. Originally, sailors who visited ____________ (1) in the South Pacific, such as the island of Tahiti, found people with designs on their bodies. ____________ (2) feel that the word originated from the Tahitian word *tatu*, meaning "to mark." The sailors brought the ____________ (3), or idea, to Europe. These men were from the lower classes, but the ____________ (4) changed and soon upper classes and royalty wanted tattoos as well. In the late 20th century, a new ____________ (5) appeared as more young people started to get tattooed. Today it doesn't matter what your profession is or what your ____________ (6) is. The desire to be a trendsetter may be ____________ (7), but tattoos are found on people across all social and ____________ (8) levels. Because of new tattooing techniques, the large, ____________ (9) designs of today cover various parts of the body and have many ____________ (10). The trend of tattooing seems to be slowing. So many people have tattoos that it no longer sets the person apart.

SECTION IV Building Vocabulary Add a suffix to the words below. In some cases, two suffixes are possible. *(2 points each)*

Noun	Verb	Adjective	Adverb
-ship -ity	-ate -ize	-ful -less	-ly

1. frequent ______
2. hope ______
3. individual ______
4. worth ______
5. special ______
6. friend ______
7. exact ______
8. secur ______
9. particip ______
10. efficient ______

Match each root word to a prefix to make one word. Write the root word on the line. *(1 point each)*

Prefix	Root Word
11. com ______	safe
12. psycho ______	bination
13. pre ______	flect
14. re ______	vent
15. un ______	logical

TOTAL ______/100 pts.

Name ____________________ Date ____________ Score __________

Volunteering in the United States

SECTION I Reading Comprehension Answer these questions about the reading passage. *(3 points each)*

A Volunteering is a practice that many people in the United States engage in at some point in their lives. It means doing unpaid work for or through an organization. It may be a simple activity, like school children cleaning up their neighborhood park, or teenagers washing cars to earn money to support their team. It may be an educational activity, like college students tutoring children after school, or professionals advising recent university graduates. It may also be for environmental organizations, like Earthwatch or Greenpeace. Whatever a person's interest, there are dozens of ways to volunteer, and many Americans do it.

B The Department of Labor collects information on volunteering in the United States, and it says that every year, over 65 million people offer their services. One-fourth of men and one-third of women work for at least one organization without being paid. The organizations that they volunteer for the most are (1) religious, (2) educational and youth services, and (3) social and community service. People between the ages of 35 and 55 tend to volunteer a great deal, but teenagers also volunteer at lot, possibly because this type of work is emphasized in schools.

C The average time spent in unpaid activities is about 50 hours per year. Retired people (over 65) offer more of their time than other age groups—over 90 hours per year. Married people tend to volunteer more than single people, and parents tend to volunteer more than adults without children. Parents are more likely to get involved in schools and sport teams, while adults without children are more likely to offer their time to hospitals or community service organizations.

D Regarding the type of work they do, people with higher levels of education are more likely to do tutoring, coaching, supervising, and counseling, or to provide management or medical assistance. Those with lower levels of education are more likely to collect, prepare, distribute, and serve food. People with full-time jobs are less likely than those with part-time jobs to volunteer. Among those who volunteered in the past but no longer do so, lack of time is the main reason, followed by health/medical problems, and family responsibilities. All in all, the trend of volunteering is alive and well in the United States, with more people lending a hand every year.

1. Volunteering may take the form of ______.
   (A) cleaning up a park
   (B) washing cars
   (C) tutoring children
   (D) all of the above

2. The number of Americans who volunteer is over ______.
   (A) 65 million
   (B) 55 million
   (C) 50 million
   (D) 35 million

3. ______ volunteer more than ______.
   (A) children / adults
   (B) married people / single people
   (C) teenagers / retired people
   (D) men / women

4. The most common type of organization to volunteer for is ______.
   (A) social
   (B) educational
   (C) religious
   (D) sports

5. In the United States, ______ people are offering their services.
   (A) not very many
   (B) the same number of
   (C) less and less
   (D) more and more

SECTION II Strategy Circle the answer that you can infer from the statement. *(3 points each)*

1. Whatever a person's interest, there are dozens of ways to volunteer, and many Americans do it.
   (A) Some people are not interested in volunteering.
   (B) There are many different organizations that people can volunteer for.
   (C) Many Americans volunteer in a dozen organizations.
   (D) It is interesting to find a dozen ways of volunteering.

2. One-fourth of men and one-third of women work for at least one organization without being paid.
   (A) Women and men volunteer in equal numbers.
   (B) More men than women volunteer.
   (C) All retired people are over 65.
   (D) All retired people have more time than other age groups.

3. Retired people (over 65) offer more of their time than other age groups—over 90 hours per year.
   (A) Older people work more unpaid hours than younger people.
   (B) Older people can only work 90 hours per year.
   (C) All retired people are over 65.
   (D) All retired people have more time than other age groups.

4. Regarding the type of work they do, people with higher levels of education are more likely to do tutoring, coaching, supervising, counseling, or provide management or medical assistance.
   (A) People with more education like teaching and sports.
   (B) People with more education like to direct other people.
   (C) People with more education know how to do medical work.
   (D) People with more education volunteer in areas where they can use the skills they have learned.

5. Among those who volunteered in the past but no longer do so, lack of time is the main reason, followed by health/medical problems, and family responsibilities.
   (A) People stop volunteering mainly because they don't have time.
   (B) People stop volunteering for dozens of reasons.
   (C) People stop volunteering because they get sick of it.
   (D) People stop volunteering because they have big families.

SECTION III New Words Complete the paragraph with words from the Academic Word List from Chapter 6. *(3 points each)*

access	areas	concept	contribute	shift
approximately	benefit	consumer	region	traditional

A volunteer organization that is very popular with young people in their 20s and 30s is Big Brother/Big Sister (BB/BS). It is a community service organization found in many __________ (1) of the U.S. The __________ (2) is very simple. It matches up boys and girls with mentors, young men and women who spend time with the children __________ (3) once or twice a month. Children who come from families that are not __________ (4), such as a two-parent family, often face obstacles. For example, the children may be alone after school or be required to take care of younger siblings. The young men and women who volunteer to be mentors get to know their Little Brother or Sister. They make it a priority to get around town with their "Littles," as they are called, and show them many different things in the __________ (5) where they live, like museums, malls, and musical performances. Under supervision of their Big Brother or Big Sister, the child learns how to be a wise __________ (6) in today's marketplace. The age gap doesn't matter, because if a person is young at heart, he or she can provide __________ (7) to a variety of interesting activities. The __________ (8) of the BB/BS program is sometimes surprising. After getting a Big Brother or Sister, there is often an amazing __________ (9) in the children's lives. Their schoolwork gets better, their self-image improves, and they look toward the future with hope. A special bond is created with their mentor, which may last a lifetime. Most importantly, they see first-hand what it means to volunteer and to __________ (10) to the well-being of others. Hopefully, the Little Brothers and Little Sisters will volunteer as Big Brothers or Big Sisters when they are adults.

SECTION IV Building Vocabulary Fill in the blanks with the correct form of the participle. *(3 points each)*

Dear Grandma,

My Big Sister took me to Disney World in Orlando for summer vacation. I was so __________ (1) (excite) when she told me we were going. We flew to Florida, and the plane ride was __________ (2) (excite). I had never been on a plane before! When we got there, we stayed at a hotel with a swimming pool. The first day I swam a lot, so I was really __________ (3) (tire) that night. The next day, we got up early and went to Disney World on a bus. In the Magic Kingdom, there were rides for children, so it was very __________ (4) (relax). Then we went to Splash Mountain, which wasn't for little kids. At first I was __________ (5) (frighten) as we rode around the mountain in a boat. All of a sudden, we were at the top and falling down! I screamed and held on to my Big Sister. But when we splashed into the water, I laughed. It was so much fun that we went again, and it was __________ (6) (thrill). Another __________ (7) (frighten) ride was Space Mountain. We went up and down and around on a small train in the dark. I was __________ (8) (terrify) the first time—and the second time, too! It was the most __________ (9) (terrify) ride I've ever been on. But then, we went back to the hotel and ate dinner by the pool. We both felt very __________ (10) (relax) after our day at Disney World. I'm so glad my Big Sister took me there!

Love,

Latisha

Write a word from Column B in Column A to form an idiom from Chapter 6. *(2 points each)*

A	B
11. went ______	clock
12. spread like ______	jerker
13. round-the- ______	viral
14. tear ______	riches
15. rags-to ______	wild fire

Name ______________________ Date ______________ Score ____________

Elephant Communication

SECTION I Reading Comprehension Answer these questions about the reading passage. *(3 points each)*

A Researchers at Stanford and Cornell Universities are studying communication patterns of the savannah, or plains, elephants, and forest elephants of sub-Saharan Africa. They have made many audio and video recordings, matching the sound and behavior of the elephants in order to understand the meaning from observed patterns.

B Their findings are that elephants use many senses to communicate: sight, smell, taste, hearing, and touch. For example, when two female elephants greet each other after a long separation, they stand side by side, flapping their ears, touching and smelling each other with their trunks, making rumbling sounds. The longer they've been separated, the louder and more demonstrative they act when they meet again.

C Elephant rumbling is a low, infrasonic sound of 12–20 Hertz (Hz) that humans cannot hear. (Human range is between 20–20,000 Hz.) Researchers have divided this rumbling into three main signals: contact, "Let's go," and mating. The contact call is used by elephants that are miles away to communicate their location to other herds. All day, female leaders rumble to other groups, who rumble back. They stay far apart to ensure enough food for all the members and later meet at a watering hole and greet each other.

D Another type of rumbling is the "Let's go" signal of a head female when she wants to leave a place after drinking or resting. Facing the direction she wants to go, she rumbles until the others begin to answer and follow her. The third type is the mating rumble that a male in musth emits. Females in a herd usually answer him, although none of them may be receptive, because they mate only once every four years. However, when the male hears them, he travels to the group to assess the situation.

E A final interesting form of communication among elephants is the way they act toward their dead. If they come upon elephant bones, they stand around touching the skulls and tusks with their trunks. When researchers left the bones of other large animals, like rhinos or buffaloes, in these places, elephants examined them briefly, but they touched only the elephant remains. In India, where elephants are often killed by trains, other elephants come to the scene to caress and mourn the dead ones.

1. Researchers are studying elephants in order to ______.
   - (A) count how many occupy a certain area
   - (B) determine how much they eat and drink
   - (C) make movies of them to show in cinemas
   - (D) understand their communication patterns

2. When female elephants greet each other after a long separation, they ______.
   (A) answer in unison and look for a male
   (B) demonstrate their excitement at meeting again
   (C) rumble and walk away
   (D) wag their trunks and tails
3. Elephant rumbling has ______.
   (A) individual meanings, depending on the elephant
   (B) no meaning
   (C) only one meaning
   (D) several meanings
4. The word emits in paragraph D probably means ______.
   (A) hears
   (B) perceives
   (C) produces
   (D) sees
5. The word remains in paragraph E is closest in meaning to ______.
   (A) bones
   (B) leaves
   (C) leftovers
   (D) stays behind

SECTION II Strategy Look back at the highlighted words and then do the activity below. *(3 points each)*

1. Rumbling is a type of elephant ______.
   (A) vocalization
   (B) body language
   (C) symbol
   (D) smell
2. An infrasonic sound is one that is ______.
   (A) too high for humans to hear
   (B) too low for humans to hear
   (C) too high for elephants to hear
   (D) too low for elephants to hear
3. The "Let's go" rumble might be given when the lead elephant ______.
   (A) has finished resting or drinking
   (B) greets another elephant
   (C) is eating
   (D) is sleeping

4. An elephant in musth is looking for another elephant ______.
   (A) to attack
   (B) to mate with
   (C) to greet
   (D) to play with

5. Elephants caress with their ______.
   (A) ears
   (B) feet
   (C) tails
   (D) trunks

SECTION III New Words Fill in the blanks with words from the Academic Word List in Chapter 7. *(3 points each)*

brains	gender	gestures	mammals	prey
shed light on	species	subjects	trails	vocalizations

Elephants are the world's largest land ______(1), weighing 5 to 7 tons, with ______(2) weighing up to 12 pounds. They travel in groups based upon ______(3), with the females of several generations forming one type of group, and young males forming another. Older males, or bulls, usually travel alone except when in *musth*. Elephant ______(4) form ancient paths through the continents of Africa and India. Zoologists used to think that there were only two ______(5) of elephants in the world, African and Asian. However, as researchers studied ______(6) on the savannahs and in the forests of Africa, they discovered that these regional types were genetically different. They also found that the elephants' ______(7) and ______(8) convey diverse messages. For example, ear flapping among females indicates friendly behavior, but among males, it indicates aggressive behavior. Different rumbles also convey different meanings. Although other animals do not ______(9) upon adult elephants, their numbers are declining because of ivory hunters and deforestation. Hopefully, current elephant communication studies will ______(10) how animal protection groups can acoustically monitor herds in certain areas and plan for conservation.

SECTION IV Building Vocabulary In the parentheses after each word, list the part of speech (n. = noun; v. = verb; adj. = adjective; adv. = adverb). Then complete the sentences that follow with the appropriate words. *(4 points each)*

1. **assess** (   ), **assessment** (   )
   A bull elephant will ________________ a herd of females to find a mate.
   If his ________________ is that none of the females is receptive, he will look for another herd.
2. **confirm** (   ), **confirmation** (   )
   A lead female makes a contact call for ________________ that other groups are in the area.
   When she receives a response, she ________________ it.
3. **demonstration** (   ), **demonstrative** (   )
   Elephant communication patterns are a ________________ of elephants' intelligence.
   When two female elephants meet after a short separation, they are less ________________.
4. **record** (   ), **recording** (   )
   Researchers are making audio and video ________________ of elephants' behavior.
   For the past few decades, they have ________________ different types of rumblings.
5. **rumble** (   ), **rumbling** (   )
   When an elephant ________________, it could be sending one of several different signals.
   The ________________ of a female who wants to leave a place is answered by her companions

TOTAL ____/100 pts.

Name ______________________ Date ______________ Score ____________

CHAPTER 8 Test

Interactions 2 Reading

Silk Production

SECTION I Reading Comprehension Answer these questions about the reading passage. *(3 points each)*

A Silk was not the main product traded on the network of caravan trails connecting East Asia to the Mediterranean Sea. Despite this fact, the German explorer, Baron Ferdinand von Richthofen, gave the Silk Road this romantic name, perhaps because it was a mysterious product. Silk-making began in China in the 3rd century B.C.E., but the process was kept a secret for several hundred years. When the Chinese merchants began trading this beautiful fabric, other countries were eager to learn how it was made.

B In the 3rd century C.E., methods of dyeing (coloring), and weaving (making cloth), were developed in a few countries along the trade routes using raw silk thread from China. In the 6th century C.E., the ruler of Constantinople asked two monks (holy men) to bring back silkworms from China. Although this was forbidden, they packed them in their bamboo canes and returned to Constantinople. There, silk production flowered and spread to Europe.

C France and Italy became centers of the European silk industry in the 15th century until a plague killed most of the silkworms in the 19th century. In the meantime, Japan had developed modern methods of making silk and soon became the world's largest producer. In the 20th century, South Korea and Thailand developed their silk industries as well.

D Sericulture, or silk production, involves cultivating thousands of tiny eggs that hatch into larvae (small worms) and feed on mulberry leaves. When the larvae grow into caterpillars (large worms), they make a cocoon (capsule) from a continuous thread that comes from the mouth and wraps around the body. Then the cocoons are steamed to kill the caterpillars and taken apart by unwinding the silk threads and twisting them together to make them stronger. Centuries ago, this work was done by hand by girls and women in silk factories, but now, it is done by machines.

E Boiling raw silk produces a lighter fabric, and the cloth can be treated with different substances so that it feels and looks different. A variety of dyeing and weaving methods produce exquisite cloth that can be made into articles of clothing. Common items include blouses, shirts, scarves, and ties of pure silk. Sweaters, jackets, coats, and hats can be made by combining silk with stronger materials for warmth. The cloth can also be used for curtains, cushions, or wall hangings in houses as decorations.

1. People wanted to learn how to make silk because ______.

Ⓐ it was a mystery

Ⓑ China kept it a secret

Ⓒ silkworms were forbidden

Ⓓ the fabric was so beautiful

2. The secret was finally brought to the West by ______.
   (A) the ruler of Constantinople
   (B) two monks traveling from China
   (C) Chinese merchants
   (D) Baron Ferdinand von Richthofen
3. The Mediterranean centers of the silk industry were ______.
   (A) South Korea and Thailand
   (B) China and Japan
   (C) Italy and France
   (D) Constantinople
4. Silk is produced by ______.
   (A) tiny eggs
   (B) worms
   (C) girls and women
   (D) machines
5. Most silk fabric is made into ______.
   (A) articles of clothing
   (B) dyeing and weaving
   (C) stronger materials
   (D) decorations

SECTION II Strategy Look back at the reading and find words with similar meanings. Then match Column A with Column B. *(2 points each)*

Column A	Column B
1. ______ caterpillars	a. capsule
2. ______ cocoon	b. cloth
3. ______ decorations	c. coloring
4. ______ dyeing	d. curtains, wall hangings
5. ______ fabric	e. food for silkworms
6. ______ larvae	f. holy men
7. ______ methods	g. industry
8. ______ monks	h. large silkworms
9. ______ mulberry leaves	i. making cloth
10. ______ network of caravan trails	j. mystery
11. ______ plague	k. sickness
12. ______ production	l. silk-making
13. ______ secret	m. Silk Road
14. ______ sericulture	n. small silkworms
15. ______ weaving	o. ways

SECTION III New Words Fill in the blanks with words from the Academic Word List from Chapter 8. *(3 points each)*

archaeologist	architecture	calligraphy	caves	depicted
frescoes	mausoleum	mosque	mummies	statues

9/19/12

Dear Françoise,

I'm on a camel tour with my classmates on part of the Silk Road, and it's really exciting! At first it was hard to ride a camel, but after a few days, I got used to it. Now it's more comfortable. Yesterday we went into some mountain ______ (1) that had pictures called ______ (2) on the walls. The paintings ______ (3) scenes of daily life in ancient times. Today we're visiting a ______ (4) in a Muslim town. The ______ (5) of the building is simple, but the Arabic ______ (6) on the walls inside is very beautiful. Our guide is an ______ (7) who is teaching us a lot about the history and culture of the Silk Road. Tomorrow, we'll stop at a ______ (8) where dead bodies were kept. There are huge carved ______ (9) representing those who died, and there are even a few ______ (10) inside. I've never seen one, so I think it will be interesting. Then we'll camp in an oasis for the night. I'm learning so much on this trip. Wish you were here!

Your cousin,

Jacques

SECTION IV Building Vocabulary Fill in the blanks with the correct words for these phrases. *(2 points each)*

1. ________________ brief, it was a wonderful trip.
2. Caravans traveled ________________ town ________________ town.
3. ________________ end, he decided to study archaeology.
4. Robbers contributed ________________ the disappearance of some art.
5. Silk was made ________________ the 15th ________________ the 19th century in Europe.
6. The artifact was ________________ the shape ________________ a pitcher.
7. The Silk Road was a network ________________ trails.

Choose the appropriate word for each sentence. *(1 point each)*

8. The cowry shells were ________________ (beautiful/good-looking).
9. The arabesques are ________________ (attractive/handsome).
10. The sick girl lost 20 pounds; she was ________________ (slim/emaciated).
11. The big jar of spices is ________________ (chubby/heavy).
12. The 300-pound man was ________________ (obese/plump).

TOTAL ____/100 pts.

Name ______________________ Date ______________ Score ____________

Disabilities

SECTION I Reading Comprehension Answer these questions about the reading passage. *(2 points each)*

A Down syndrome (DS) is a genetic disorder caused by an extra chromosome. Humans normally have 23 pairs of chromosomes, or 46; however, people with DS have 47. These infants typically have a wide face, short neck, slanted eyes, and are mentally retarded, that is, with low intelligence. They are likely to have kidney or heart problems, and adults rarely live beyond 50 years, but they are generally happy people with optimistic personalities.

B It is possible for a woman of any age to have a baby with DS, but it occurs more often in older women. For all women, the rate is one baby with DS out of 800 born, but this increases to one out of 80 for women over 35. So doctors suggest that women in this age group get tested for the condition if they become pregnant. Besides DS, there are several other disabilities that are caused by "mistakes" in our genes.

C Years ago, children with disabilities couldn't attend public schools or get jobs. They usually went to institutions where they were kept for the rest of their lives. However, attitudes have changed in recent decades, thanks to parents with disabled children. In 1975, a law called Individuals with Disabilities Education Act (IDEA) was passed in the United States. This law stated that all children with physical and mental disabilities had the right to an education, so schools were required to offer classes to meet their needs. Colleges began offering courses in "special education" to train teachers in new methods.

D This change in attitude made it possible for children with disabilities to get an education. Parents formed support groups, helping each other find good schools, recreation activities, and sports centers for their children. No longer were these children kept at home or in institutions. They could go to school with normal children and learn—and later be trained to do simple work and earn money. They could then live in group homes and support themselves like other people.

E In 1968, the Special Olympics, a competition for children and adults with disabilities, were held for the first time in Chicago, Illinois, with 1,000 participants. Today they are held every other year, with 2.25 million athletes participating in 150 countries around the world. People with disabilities are no longer ignored or institutionalized; they are part of a lively community of special people who are now able to contribute to society.

1. People with Down syndrome ________.

   (A) have a wide face

   (B) have slanted eyes

   (C) are mentally retarded

   (D) all of the above

2. More babies with DS are born to ________.
   (A) women of any age
   (B) women over 35
   (C) women over 80
   (D) over 800 women
3. IDEA, the law passed in 1975, stated that ________.
   (A) all children with disabilities had a right to an education
   (B) some schools were required to offer special classes
   (C) colleges had to teach special education
   (D) teachers had to learn new methods
4. Because of special education, children grew up and ________.
   (A) could support themselves
   (B) had to be kept at home
   (C) had to be kept in institutions
   (D) had to learn as much as normal children
5. The Special Olympics ________.
   (A) is always held in Chicago
   (B) has 1,000 participants
   (C) has millions of participants
   (D) was held once in 1968

SECTION II Strategy For each statement below, write *fact* or *assumption*, according to the presentation of information in the reading selection. *(3 points each)*

1. ______________ Down syndrome is a genetic disorder caused by an extra chromosome.
2. ______________ There is physical evidence of DS, like slanted eyes and a wide face.
3. ______________ Adults with DS don't live long because of heart and kidney problems.
4. ______________ Women over the age of 35 have a higher chance of having a baby with DS.
5. ______________ Pregnant women over 35 always get tested for DS.
6. ______________ Children with disabilities had to live in institutions before 1975.
7. ______________ All children with disabilities must be educated today.
8. ______________ Most people with disabilities live in group homes.
9. ______________ The Special Olympics are only for people with disabilities.
10. ______________ These games are held in many countries around the world today.

SECTION III New Words Fill in the blanks with words from the Academic Word List from Chapter 9. *(3 points each)*

cognitive	colleagues	identity	intuition	involved
maturation	memory	neuroscientist	psychologist	researchers

7/17/12

Dear Rosemary,

As you know, I've been looking for my identical twin sister for years, and I finally found her! Just as psychologists predict, we have many similarities. As you know, I've been ______(1) with work on the science of the brain. As a ______(2) I've studied long-term ______(3), or how adults remember events from childhood. Well, my sister is a ______(4) studying the same area, but with children. She wants to find out how memory changes with ______(5), or how the early memories of children and teenagers differ. We met by accident at a conference on ______(6) science. There were many ______(7) there, and one of my ______(8) from the institute told me she had seen a woman who looked exactly like me. I went to the room where this woman was giving a presentation. I didn't want to bother her, so I hid my ______(9) by sitting in the back. Her presentation was interesting, and afterward, I went to the front of the room. She looked at me without saying a word—then we just hugged each other. She said that her ______(10) told her that we'd find each other soon. It's incredible, but I feel like I've known her all my life. She's coming to my house for dinner now; we both love to cook. More later!

Your friend,

Connie

SECTION IV Building Vocabulary Circle the correct word in each sentence. *(3 points each)*

1. A region in the hypothalamus is larger in (heterosexual / homosexual) men than in women and gay men.
2. The brain is divided into two (atmospheres / hemispheres).
3. When we dream, we sometimes have (insights / outsights) about our lives.
4. It is possible to have (pressed / repressed) memories.
5. Child- teenager- adult: this is the (chronology / geology) of a human life.
6. The word (vibraphone / telephone) means to "hear at a distance."
7. A (microscope / microwave) allows us to see small organisms.
8. A man who has many wives is a (bigamist / polygamist).
9. Some people who meditate practice (Buddhism / Buddhist).
10. We have 23 pairs of (homophones / chromosomes).

TOTAL ____/100 pts.

Name ______________________ Date ______________ Score ______________

The Graduation Ceremony

SECTION I Reading Comprehension Answer these questions about the reading passage. *(2 points each)*

A Graduating from college is a rite of passage from adolescence to adulthood for many young people. After finishing high school, teenagers begin their studies and emerge from the university as young adults. At first, they may not be sure of what to study, but after two years, they decide on a major. Then they have to take the required courses and get good grades. If they pass all their exams, they receive a bachelor's degree.

B The graduation ceremony marks the culmination of four years of study, and most universities require students to wear a cap, a kind of "hat," and a gown, a kind of robe. This type of dress was common in the 13th century when people wore it to keep warm in cold buildings. Now students wear it only at graduation, and each college has special colors that identify not only their players at sports events but also their graduates.

C A few weeks before graduation, students rent or buy a cap and gown from the university. They send invitations to family and friends to join them in celebrating the end of several years of hard work. On the big day, the graduates march into an auditorium or onto a football field in their colorful robes often to the music of "Pomp and Circumstance" by Sir Edward Elgar. Famous people give speeches to encourage the graduates to use their education for the good of society. They receive diplomas stating that they have earned a degree, and the university president officially declares them graduates. While proud parents wipe tears from their eyes, graduates begin cheering and tossing their caps in the air on this happy occasion.

D At some universities, it is common for graduating students to plan "pranks," or acts that are not usually permitted. These range from simple ones—like putting soap in a campus fountain to make bubbles—to complex ones, like putting a car on the roof of a building. In 2006, students from the Massachusetts Institute of Technology (MIT) went to the California Institute of Technology (CalTech) and "stole" a famous symbol. It was a cannon weighing 1.7 tons that had been used in the Spanish-American War. MIT students delivered it to their campus 3,000 miles away where they proudly displayed it—until some CalTech students came to "rescue" it a week later and take it home.

1. Students can graduate from college if they ______.

(A) put soap in the fountain

(B) march to music

(C) steal a cannon

(D) pass their exams

2. Students wear caps and gowns today because ________.
   (A) it is cold in the buildings
   (B) it is a tradition
   (C) they are colorful
   (D) they are warm
3. Families want to celebrate the graduates' ________.
   (A) pranks
   (B) tears
   (C) cheering
   (D) hard work
4. An example of a simple prank is ________.
   (A) putting a car on the roof
   (B) stealing a cannon
   (C) putting soap in a fountain
   (D) returning a cannon
5. Next time, CalTech may ________.
   (A) plan a prank at MIT
   (B) take back their cannon
   (C) transport the cannon to Spain
   (D) rescue MIT students

SECTION II Strategy For each statement below, write *fact* or *opinion*, according to the presentation of information in the reading selection. *(3 points each)*

1. ______________ The majority students are adolescents when they begin college and young adults when they finish.
2. ______________ It's impossible to decide what subject to study when you're 18.
3. ______________ Nowadays, students don't like to wear caps and gowns.
4. ______________ Graduating students usually invite their families to the ceremony.
5. ______________ The speeches that famous people give at the ceremony are boring.
6. ______________ Diplomas state that students have earned a degree from the university.
7. ______________ Most graduates are sad to leave college and get a job.
8. ______________ Some students plan pranks around the time of graduation.
9. ______________ Stealing a cannon and transporting it 3,000 miles is a complex prank.
10. ______________ Students who carry out pranks should be punished.

SECTION III New Words Fill in the blanks with words from the Academic Word List from Chapter 10. *(3 points each)*

ask for	coming-of-age	corporation	guidance	negotiations
previous	proposal	regain	rite of passage	vision

4/14/12

Dear Julio,

It's been five years since we graduated, but I still miss my old friends from college. That's why the reunion of the Class of 2007 this summer is going to be great! The years at Central State University were the best years of our lives. It was a ______(1)______ period in which we were growing from adolescence to adulthood. We were leaving behind our ______(2)______ friends from high school and finding new ones in college. We were trying to decide who we were and what we wanted to do, to develop a ______(3)______ for the future. We took courses and looked for ______(4)______ from our professors, hoping they would help us decide on a profession. I remember a ______(5)______ from one of my professors; she said that how much money you made wasn't as important as how much better you made the world. At first, I was just concerned about paying back my student loans to the bank. I wanted to ______(6)______ a sense of independence, of not owing money to anyone. When I paid them back, I remembered my professor's advice about contributing to society. I decided to work for a nonprofit ______(7)______. I got a job with Fair Trade, an organization that buys food products, like coffee, from small farmers. These farmers can't ______(8)______ high prices because they produce small crops. So Fair Trade holds ______(9)______ with food companies so that they pay fair prices to the farmers. I even went to Central America to visit these farms, which was like a ______(10)______ for me. I realized how much I really have and how much I must give back to society.

Your friend,

Shawn

SECTION IV Building Vocabulary Circle the correct word in each sentence. *(3 points each)*

1. A diploma is (inspired / inscribed) with a student's name.
2. People who attend the same university have a common spirit, or (esprit de corps / esprit de mort).
3. When a group of people share a certain, usually traditional, set of beliefs, we say they are (orthosox / orthodox).
4. Students who study hard are usually (productive / inductive) later in life.
5. If a man has two wives, he is considered a (bigamist / polygamist) in some countries.
6. The process of breathing is called (perspiration / respiration).
7. In a trial, the (proceedings / decedents) are recorded by a court secretary.
8. Romeo and Juliet had a love that was (remorseful / immortal).
9. A college student's record of courses and grades is called a (postscript / transcript).
10. During a funeral in some cultures, the (corpse / corporation) is burned.

TOTAL ____/100 pts.

Chapter 1 Test Answer Key

Section I

1. A 2. B 3. B
4. D 5. A

Section II

1. D 2. B 3. C
4. B 5. D

Section III

1. resources 2. identical 3. assignments
4. required 5. challenging 6. isolated 7. achieve
8. credits 9. status 10. obvious

Section IV

1. into 2. to 3. in, to 4. one, about 5. other
6. to 7. For 8. up

Chapter 2 Test Answer Key

Section I

1. B 2. D 3. A
4. A 5. C

Section II

1. h 2. j 3. f 4. g 5. i
6. c 7. e 8. a 9. d 10. b

Section III

1. environment 2. transportation 3. global
4. residents 5. method 6. established 7. predict
8. focused 9. access 10. solve

Section IV

1. differ 2. differently 3. pollution 4. polluted
5. predict 6. predictably 7. safety 8. safe
9. solution 10. solvable 11. different
12. predictable 13. solution 14. pollute 15. safely

Chapter 3 Test Answer Key

Section I

1. A 2. C 3. D 4. B 5. A

Section II

1. C 2. C 3. A 4. A 5. D

Section III

1. common knowledge 2. item 3. influenced
4. success 5. funds 6. grants 7. sport utility vehicle 8. capacity 9. economy 10. consumes

Section IV

1. *n.* 2. *adj.* 3. *adj.* 4. *n.* 5. *adj.* 6. *n.* 7. *n.*
8. *adj.* 9. *adj.* 10. *n.* 11. Marketers 12. offensive
13. dissatisfaction 14. information 15. advantage
16. identical 17. violent 18. subsidiary
19. influential 20. social

Chapter 4 Test Answer Key

Section I

1. B 2. D 3. C
4. A 5. C

Section II

1. D 2. C 3. A
4. B 5. B

Section III

1. on the move 2. outsourcing 3. overworked
4. stress 5. upgrade 6. keep up with
7. career counselors 8. job security 9. leisure
10. telecommuting

Section IV

1. manufacturing 2. classified 3. hopping
4. confidence 5. part 6. drawbacks 7. agencies
8. workforce 9. personnel 10. worldwide

Chapter 5 Test Answer Key

Section I

1. D 2. C 3. A
4. B 5. C

Section II

1. d 2. j 3. e 4. a 5. g
6. i 7. f 8. b 9. h 10. c

Section III

1. areas 2. Researchers 3. concept
4. environment 5. trend 6. income 7. psychological
8. economic 9. complex 10. components

Section IV

1. frequently 2. hopeful/hopeless 3. individuality/individually 4. worthless 5. specialize/specially
6. friendship/friendly 7. exactly 8. security
9. participate 10. efficiently 11. combination
12. psychological 13. prevent 14. reflect
15. unsafe

Chapter 6 Test Answer Key

Section I

1. D 2. A 3. B
4. C 5. D

Section II

1. B 2. C 3. A
4. D 5. A

Section III

1. areas/regions **2.** concept **3.** approximately
4. traditional **5.** areas/regions **6.** consumer
7. access **8.** benefit **9.** shift **10.** contribute

Section IV

1. excited **2.** exciting **3.** tired **4.** relaxing
5. frightened **6.** thrilling **7.** frightening **8.** terrified
9. terrifying **10.** relaxed **11.** went viral
12. spread like wild fire **13.** round-the-clock
14. tearjerker **15.** rags-to-riches

Chapter 7 Test Answer Key

Section I

1. D **2.** B **3.** D
4. C **5.** A

Section II

1. A **2.** B **3.** A
4. B **5.** D

Section III

1. mammals **2.** brains **3.** gender **4.** trails
5. species **6.** subjects **7.** gestures **8.** vocalizations
9. prey **10.** shed light on

Section IV

1. *v.*, *n.*, assess, assessment
2. *v.*, *n.*, confirmation, confirms
3. *n.*, *adj.*, demonstration, demonstrative
4. *v.*, n., recordings, recorded
5. v., *n.*, rumbles, rumbling

Chapter 8 Test Answer Key

Section I

1. D **2.** B **3.** C **4.** B **5.** A

Section II

1. h **2.** a **3.** d **4.** c **5.** b **6.** n **7.** o **8.** f
9. e **10.** m **11.** k **12.** g **13.** j **14.** l **15.** i

Section III

1. caves **2.** frescoes **3.** depicted **4.** mosque
5. architecture **6.** calligraphy **7.** archaeologist
8. mausoleum **9.** statues **10.** mummies

Section IV

1. In **2.** from/to **3.** To this **4.** to **5.** from/to
6. in/of **7.** of **8.** beautiful **9.** attractive
10. emaciated **11.** heavy **12.** obese

Chapter 9 Test Answer Key

Section I

1. D **2.** B **3.** A **4.** A **5.** C

Section II

1. fact **2.** fact **3.** assumption **4.** fact
5. assumption **6.** assumption **7.** fact
8. assumption **9.** fact **10.** fact

Section III

1. involved **2.** neuroscientist **3.** memory
4. psychologist **5.** maturation **6.** cognitive
7. researchers **8.** colleagues **9.** identity
10. intuition

Section IV

1. heterosexual **2.** hemispheres **3.** insights
4. repressed **5.** chronology **6.** telephone
7. microscope **8.** polygamist **9.** Buddhism
10. chromosomes

Chapter 10 Test Answer Key

Section I

1. D **2.** B **3.** D **4.** C **5.** A

Section II

1. fact **2.** opinion **3.** opinion **4.** fact **5.** opinion
6. fact **7.** opinion **8.** fact **9.** fact **10.** opinion

Section III

1. coming-of-age **2.** previous **3.** vision **4.** guidance
5. proposal **6.** regain **7.** corporation **8.** ask for
9. negotiations **10.** rite of passage

Section IV

1. inscribed **2.** esprit de corps **3.** orthodox
4. productive **5.** bigamist **6.** respiration
7. proceedings **8.** immortal **9.** transcript
10. corpse

Name ______________________ Date ______________ Score ______________

PLACEMENT **Test** **INTERACTIONS/MOSAIC** Reading

VOCABULARY I Choose the best word to complete each sentence. *(2 points each)*

Example Brazil and Argentina are the largest ______ in South America.

(A) categories
(B) cities
(C) countries
(D) neighborhoods

1. No one lives with Rosa in her apartment. She lives ______.
   (A) alone
   (B) lonely
   (C) only
   (D) together

2. Tom's family has 3 children, Amy's family has 3 children, Reina's family has 2 children, and Ben's family has 2 children. The ______ number of children in these families is 2.5.
   (A) small
   (B) average
   (C) equal
   (D) total

3. When teachers speak too softly and rapidly, it is ______ for their students to understand them.
   (A) easy
   (B) little
   (C) different
   (D) difficult

4. In many cultures, women do most of the ______. For example, they clean the floors and wash the clothes for their families.
   (A) farming
   (B) homework
   (C) housework
   (D) cooking

5. Mr. Lee's restaurant is successful because he always waits on his ______ politely and serves them wonderful meals.
   (A) customs
   (B) customers
   (C) consumers
   (D) users

6. In a basketball game, two teams _______ against each other to score points by throwing a ball into a basket.

(A) compete
(B) cooperate
(C) complete
(D) exercise

7. In this country doctors usually have high _______, or position in the society.

(A) profession
(B) situation
(C) state
(D) status

8. Many companies in the computer industry were started by very young people. For example, Bill Gates was only twenty years old when he and Paul Allen _______ the Microsoft Corporation in 1975.

(A) based
(B) discovered
(C) located
(D) founded

9. _______ up to 20% is customary in U.S. restaurants. Some places even add 15% to the bill for all parties of six or more.

(A) Waiting
(B) Tipping
(C) Buying
(D) Eating

10. I wouldn't go to the new mall just yet. If you can _______ another week or two, until the Grand Opening is over, the crowds will be much more manageable.

(A) hold out
(B) hold up
(C) wait on
(D) hold onto

VOCABULARY II Read each item and then answer the vocabulary question below it. *(2 points each)*

Example The city government recently announced plans to build a new road through Mountain Dale, a beautiful neighborhood on the south side of the city. The residents of Mountain Dale are angry about the road. Yesterday a group of them went to a meeting at City Hall to express their *views* on the city's plans.

Which of the following is closest in meaning to *views* as it is used above?

(A) pictures
(B) opinions
(C) sights
(D) beautiful scenery

1. The brain is divided into many parts. Each part serves specific and important functions. The cerebrum is the largest and most complex *area* of the brain. It controls thought, learning, and many other activities.

   Which of the following is closest in meaning to *area* as it is used above?

   (A) the size of a surface, calculated by multiplying the length by the width
   (B) a particular subject or group of related subjects
   (C) a particular part or section
   (D) a part of an activity or a thought

2. By studying the pyramids of Egypt, researchers have learned a great deal about ancient Egyptian *culture*. They have discovered, for example, that different social classes existed even in the earliest cities.

   Which of the following is closest in meaning to *culture* as it is used above?

   (A) activities that are related to art, music, and literature
   (B) a society that existed at a particular time in history
   (C) a scientific experiment of people from a particular country
   (D) education of people in a certain social group

3. Timothy is going to ride his bike around the world. In order to see all the countries and sights he wants to, before he begins his adventure, he will *map* his route.

   Which of the following is the closest in meaning to *map* as used above?

   (A) to pack bags for a trip
   (B) to plan the path of a trip
   (C) to prepare a bicycle for a trip
   (D) to talk about something

4. With today's computer networks, the *transmission* of data from one place in the world to another can happen instantly.

   Which of the following is closest in meaning to *transmission* as it is used above?

   (A) the process of working together on the same computer network
   (B) a job that involves traveling from one place to another
   (C) the set of parts of a vehicle that take power from the engine to the wheels
   (D) the process of sending information using electronic equipment

5. Roger has some annoying tendencies. For one thing, he's *inclined* to talk about himself and his achievements.

   Which of the following is closest in meaning to *inclined* as it is used above?

   (A) bending forward to say something
   (B) likely to do something or behave in a particular way
   (C) holding a particular opinion
   (D) talking a lot about the same thing

6. At medical centers throughout the United States, researchers are *conducting* investigations into the causes of heart disease.

Which of the following is closest in meaning to *conducting* as it is used above?

(A) carrying out an activity or process in order to get information or prove facts
(B) directing the playing of an orchestra, band, etc.
(C) carrying something like electricity or heat to cure heart disease
(D) guiding or leading someone somewhere

7. In recent years, it seems that headlines and articles about war and violence have *occupied* the front pages of newspapers everywhere.

Which of the following is closest in meaning to *occupied* as it is used above?

(A) taken up time
(B) lived in a place
(C) controlled a place by military force
(D) filled a particular amount of space

8. Studies in public schools have shown that *exposure* to art and music has many benefits for children. It improves their literacy, critical thinking, and math skills.

Which of the following is closest in meaning to *exposure* as it is used above?

(A) a situation in which someone is not protected from risk or danger
(B) attention that someone gets from newspapers, television, etc.
(C) the chance to experience something
(D) the act of showing something that is usually hidden

9. Ronald and James are roommates in a university dormitory. They have frequent arguments because Ronald prefers to go to sleep early and James always stays up late. Also, Ronald likes quiet while he studies, but James insists that loud music helps him concentrate. How can James and Ronald *resolve* these conflicts?

Which of the following is closest in meaning to *resolve* as it is used above?

(A) make a definite decision to do something
(B) solve again using new techniques
(C) gradually change into something else
(D) find a satisfactory way of dealing with a problem or difficulty

10. It is important that students learn to read and write before they go to college. In particular, they need to practice reading on their own and learn how to write a *succinct* and logical argument.

Which of the following is the closest in meaning to *succinct* as used above?

(A) taking a long time to explain
(B) correct
(C) original
(D) clearly and concisely expressed

Reading Section

DIRECTIONS: Read each passage and answer the questions below it. *(2 points each)*

Reading Passage 1

A How do you react to the taste of different foods, like coffee or lemon? Do they have a flavor that you like? Or do they taste very strong to you? Why do people react differently to different flavors?

B We all know that different people have different food preferences. Researchers have discovered some reasons for these differences. Your culture and your life experience are partly responsible for your preferences for certain foods. Your food preferences are also partly genetic. (Your genetic preferences are the ones that you were born with.) In order to discover people's genetic preferences, researchers use a chemical called PROP. People taste it and respond to the taste. To some people, PROP has no flavor. The researchers classify these people as "nontasters." To other people, the flavor of PROP is a little bitter, or sharp. These people are "tasters." Then there are the people who can't stand the flavor of PROP. They find it to be unbearably bitter. These people are the "supertasters." Tasters have more taste buds on their tongues than nontasters do, and supertasters have many more taste buds than tasters do. This explains why supertasters are more sensitive to PROP and to the flavors in certain foods. So if you think the flavors in coffee, grapefruit juice, and broccoli are very strong, you may be a "supertaster."

Example The topic of the reading passage is ______.

- (A) the flavor of coffee
- (B) becoming a supertaster
- (C) differences in people's taste sensitivity
- (D) research in the flavor of different foods

1. The main idea of the reading is that ______.
   - (A) there are people who like different foods
   - (B) there are cultural and genetic reasons for the differences in people's food preferences
   - (C) some foods have a very strong flavor
   - (D) PROPs can be used to identify different types of tastes
2. The meaning of *genetic* preferences is ______.
   - (A) preferences for certain foods
   - (B) preferences researchers have discovered
   - (C) the preferences of some people
   - (D) the preferences that people are born with
3. What is PROP?
   - (A) a chemical
   - (B) something that people are born with
   - (C) a discovery
   - (D) a researcher

4. Why do researchers use PROP?

- (A) because it has no flavor
- (B) to find out the responses to foods people were born with
- (C) to discover the flavors in certain foods
- (D) because people like its flavor

5. A food that is bitter has ______.

- (A) no flavor
- (B) little flavor
- (C) a coffee flavor
- (D) a sharp flavor

6. People who ______ are classified as *supertasters.*

- (A) can't stand the flavor of PROP
- (B) think that PROP has no flavor
- (C) think that PROP tastes a little bitter
- (D) like bitter flavors

7. Taste buds are probably ______.

- (A) tiny pieces of food
- (B) the small bumps on the surface of people's tongues
- (C) chemicals in food that give it its flavor
- (D) something in broccoli, grapefruit juice, and coffee

Reading Passage 2

A After a cold, snowy winter, many people look forward to the long hot days of summer. The normal heat of summer can be pleasant. However, it's important to be aware that excessive—that is, too much—heat can be dangerous. There are other summer weather dangers, for example, tornadoes, lightning, and floods, but excessive heat kills more people each year than any of these. According to meteorologists (weather scientists), a heat wave is a period of excessive heat that lasts two days or more. A heat wave stresses people and can cause illnesses. These illnesses include heat cramps, heat exhaustion, and heat stroke. The people who are at the greatest risk during heat waves are the elderly, babies, and those with serious diseases.

B High humidity (moisture in the air) can make the effects of heat even more harmful. As humidity increases, the air seems warmer than it actually is because it's more difficult for the body to cool itself through the evaporation of perspiration. During heat waves, meteorologists use the heat index to determine the level of danger. The heat index measures how hot it really feels when high humidity is added to the actual air temperature. As an example, if the air temperature is 95° F (Fahrenheit) and the humidity is 35%, the heat index is 98° F. But if the air temperature is 95° F and the humidity is 70%, the heat index is 124° F. Doctors say that even young, healthy people can die of heat stroke if they exercise outside when the heat index is high. During a heat wave, it's best to take it easy, drink plenty of water, and stay out of the heat as much as possible.

1. The main idea of Paragraph A is that ______.
   (A) people look forward to the long hot days of summer
   (B) too much heat can have dangerous effects
   (C) tornadoes, lightning, and floods are dangerous
   (D) meteorologists can define heat waves
2. The main idea of Paragraph B is that ______.
   (A) humidity is moisture in the air
   (B) meteorologists use the heat index during heat waves
   (C) high humidity increases the danger of high air temperatures
   (D) it's important to stay inside during a heat wave
3. The word *excessive* means ______.
   (A) too much
   (B) important
   (C) long
   (D) coming in waves
4. In the passage, lightning is mentioned as an example of ______.
   (A) excessive heat
   (B) a storm
   (C) a stress on people
   (D) a summer weather danger
5. A meteorologist is ______.
   (A) a doctor
   (B) a weather scientist
   (C) a space scientist
   (D) a dangerous weather condition
6. The heat index measures ______.
   (A) the amount of moisture in the air
   (B) air temperature
   (C) a person's body temperature
   (D) the temperature the body feels when heat and humidity are combined
7. Based on the information in the passage, which statement is true?
   (A) Young, healthy people are more likely to die from excessive heat than elderly people are.
   (B) The elderly, babies, and people with serious diseases are most likely to die from excessive heat, but it can kill young, healthy people, too.
   (C) Perspiration is a dangerous effect of excessive heat.
   (D) All heat waves include high humidity.

8. Why did the author write this passage?

(A) To warn people about the dangers of excessive heat and give suggestions about avoiding them.

(B) To give people useful information about the weather in the summer.

(C) To describe the work of meteorologists and their use of the heat index.

(D) To let people know how the body can cool itself naturally.

Reading Passage 3

A Even though education is compulsory (required by law) for children in the United States, it is not compulsory for them to go to a conventional school to get that education. In every one of the 50 states, it is legal for parents to educate their children at home, or to "home school" their children. Although no state requires parents to have special training to home school their children, the regulations parents must follow vary widely from state to state. New Jersey, for example, imposes virtually no requirements. In contrast, New York requires home schoolers to notify their school districts, file instructional plans and frequent reports, and submit the results of tests or other forms of assessment for each child.

B Increasing numbers of American families have been opting for home schooling. According to the National Center for Educational Statistics, about 1.1 million children were being home schooled in the spring of 2003. This represents an increase from the 850,000 who were being home schooled in the spring of 1999. In addition, the home-schooling rate—the percentage of the school-age population that was being home schooled—increased from 1.7 percent in 1999 to 2.2 percent in 2003.

C A survey conducted in 2003 asked parents to give their most important reasons for home schooling their children. Thirty-one percent cited concerns about the environment in conventional schools, including safety, drugs, or negative peer pressure. Thirty percent said that the most important reason was to provide religious or moral instruction. Sixteen percent said that the most important reason was dissatisfaction with academic instruction at conventional schools. Parents gave other reasons, too; for instance, many said that they wanted to strengthen family bonds or allow their children more freedom.

D It is difficult to show whether conventional schooling or home schooling works better. Home-schooled children tend to score significantly higher than the national average on college entrance tests. But educators say that it isn't easy to determine how meaningful the figures are, given the complexities of making direct comparisons. In the debate about home schooling, socialization is more of an issue than achievement. Advocates of conventional education believe that home-schooled children are at a disadvantage because they miss out on the kinds of social interaction and relationships with peers that are an essential part of a total education. Advocates of home schooling say that home-schooled children are not socially isolated; they think that home-schooled children have a larger social structure because they can be out in the world, in contact with people of different ages, and having experiences that they could never have in conventional schools.

DIRECTIONS: For each question, choose the best answer based on the reading passage.

1. The word *conventional* means ________.

(A) relating to a meeting

(B) following what is normal or usual

(C) following a religion

(D) educational

2. According to the passage, increasing numbers of American families are choosing home schooling. What information does the author give to support this statement?
   - (A) In every one of the 50 states, it is legal for parents to educate their children at home.
   - (B) Thirty-one percent of parents say that the most important reason for home schooling is concerns about the environment in conventional schools.
   - (C) The number of children who were being home schooled increased from 850,000 in 1999 to about 1.1 million in 2003.
   - (D) A survey was conducted in 2003.

3. Scan (look quickly through) the passage to find the answer to this question: How many of the parents surveyed in 2003 said that the most important reason for home schooling their children was dissatisfaction with academic instruction at conventional schools?
   - (A) 1.1 million
   - (B) 30 percent
   - (C) 16 percent
   - (D) 2.2 percent

4. Three of the following statements give facts, and one gives an opinion. Based on the reading passage, which one is the opinion?
   - (A) Home-schooled children are at a disadvantage because they miss out on some kinds of social interaction and relationships.
   - (B) Thirty percent of parents who home school their children said that the most important reason was to provide religious or moral instruction.
   - (C) The home-schooling rate increased from 1.7 percent in 1999 to 2.2 percent in 2003.
   - (D) The regulations that parents of home schoolers must follow vary widely from state to state.

5. Which paragraph gives information about the number of home-schooled children who attend college?
   - (A) Paragraph B
   - (B) Paragraph C
   - (C) Paragraph D
   - (D) That information is not given in the passage.

6. In Paragraph D, the author implies, but does not state directly, that ______.
   - (A) home-schooled children tend to score significantly higher than the national average on college entrance tests
   - (B) it should be easy to make direct comparisons between conventional and home schooling
   - (C) parents are not academically qualified to teach their children
   - (D) there is controversy about the benefits of home schooling

7. Based on Paragraph D, we can conclude that advocates of conventional education object to home schooling mainly because home-schooled children ______.
   - (A) cannot achieve academically
   - (B) cannot be compared to conventionally educated children
   - (C) are not well socialized
   - (D) have too much freedom

Reading Passage 4

A In recent years, the game of golf and golf tourism have grown in popularity in many places in the world. Golf, which traces its roots back to 15th century Scotland, is often viewed as a pleasant and harmless way to relax in a natural setting. But golf courses are not natural developments. They are artificial constructions that have a big environmental impact. As a result, there is often controversy about the building of golf courses.

B Opponents of the use of land for golf courses bring up a number of environmental concerns. One is that a golf course covers a great deal of land, typically up to 200 acres, and in the process of developing this land into a golf course, it is common for fragile native ecosystems such as wetlands, rainforests, or coastal dunes to be destroyed. Indigenous grasses, shrubs, and trees are removed and replaced by foreign vegetation. The construction process causes soil erosion and results in the loss of biodiversity and habitat for wildlife. Another concern is the amount of chemical pesticides, herbicides, and fertilizers used to maintain the grass on a golf course once it is established. These chemicals can result in toxic contamination of the air, the soil, the surface water, and the underground water, and this in turn leads to health problems for people who live near the course or downstream from it, for people who work at the course, and even for the golfers. Yet another concern is that golf courses require an enormous amount of water every day. Their water consumption can lead to depletion of scarce fresh water resources. These and other concerns about golf courses have provoked protests, most recently in east and southeast Asia, against planned golf projects.

C Designers, developers, and operators of golf courses have become increasingly aware of the environmental issues and of the protests. Consequently, they have sponsored research into more environmentally sensitive ways of constructing and maintaining courses. They believe that it is possible to build golf courses which protect and preserve the natural features of the landscape and natural habitats for wildlife. Their suggested practices include using native trees and shrubs, planting types of grass that require less water and are best adapted to the local climate, and using reclaimed water. Proponents of golf courses believe that these "green" golf courses can actually provide environmental benefits to their sites.

D However, even a "green" golf course is likely to result in some environmental degradation and loss of habitat. Therefore, many biologists and wildlife ecologists, such as Lawrence Woolbright, a professor at Siena College in Albany, New York, contend that the best places to construct new golf courses are places that are already degraded, such as former landfills (garbage dumps) and old industrial sites, rather than on undeveloped land. A golf course that transforms a degraded site into a scenic landscape with wetlands and woodlands and habitat for wildlife could actually be a benefit to the environment.

1. Which of the following is the best statement of the main idea of the reading passage?

(A) Golf courses are artificial constructions, and are often built with no regard for the environment.

(B) Controversies about golf courses affect the tourist trade.

(C) Golf courses have significant effects on the environment, and these effects lead to controversy.

(D) Golf and golf tourism are growing in popularity internationally, leading to a more negative effect on the environment.

2. What word is opposite in meaning to the word *indigenous*?

(A) native
(B) foreign
(C) natural
(D) vegetation

3. Which of the following is *not* mentioned in the passage as a negative environmental impact of a golf course?

(A) the destruction of fragile native ecosystems
(B) soil erosion caused by cutting down trees
(C) pollution caused by traffic and maintenance equipment
(D) depletion of scarce fresh water resources

4. Which of the following best summarizes the environmental concerns of opponents of the use of land for golf courses?

(A) They are concerned about the amount of land that a golf course covers.
(B) They are concerned about the impact of the process of constructing new golf courses.
(C) They are concerned about the impact of the maintenance of established golf courses.
(D) All of the above.

5. Based on Paragraphs C and D, we can infer that a "green" golf course is one that ________.

(A) consumes a great deal of water
(B) is environmentally sensitive
(C) is new and not degraded
(D) has grass, shrubs, and trees

6. Based on the information in Paragraph C, we can conclude that ________.

(A) it is certain that "green" golf courses have already been built
(B) it is certain that "green" golf courses will be built in the future
(C) it is not certain that any "green" golf courses have already been built or will be built in the future
(D) opponents of golf courses accept the idea that "green" golf courses can actually provide environmental benefits to their sites

7. Based on Paragraph D, we can infer that the author of the passage ________.

(A) agrees with Lawrence Woolbright
(B) disagrees with Lawrence Woolbright
(C) is willing to accept some environmental degradation and loss of habitat
(D) is opposed to all golf courses

8. What would be an appropriate title for this reading passage?

(A) A Brief History of Golf
(B) Golf's Dirty Side
(C) Why Make Golf Green?
(D) The Beauty of Golf

Interactions/Mosaic Reading Placement Test Answer Key

Vocabulary I

1. A **2.** B **3.** D **4.** C **5.** B
6. A **7.** D **8.** D **9.** B **10.** A

Vocabulary II

1. C **2.** B **3.** B **4.** D **5.** B
6. A **7.** D **8.** C **9.** D **10.** D

Reading Passage 1

1. B **2.** D **3.** A **4.** B **5.** D **6.** A **7.** B

Reading Passage 2

1. B **2.** C **3.** A **4.** D **5.** B **6.** D **7.** B **8.** B

Reading Passage 3

1. B **2.** C **3.** C **4.** A **5.** D **6.** D **7.** C

Reading Passage 4

1. C **2.** B **3.** C **4.** D **5.** B **6.** C **7.** A **8.** C

SCORING FOR INTERACTIONS/MOSAIC READING PLACEMENT TEST	
Score	**Placement**
0–40	Interactions Access
41–55	Interactions 1
56–70	Interactions 2
71–85	Mosaic 1
86–100	Mosaic 2

This is a rough guide. Teachers should use their judgment in placing students and selecting texts.